WHAT'S ON THE
OTHER SIDE?

OTHER TITLES BY BRENT L. TOP

Books

Doctrinal Commentary on the Book of Mormon, vols. 1–4
(with Robert L. Millet and Joseph Fielding McConkie)

*Follow the Living Prophets: Timely Reasons for
Observing Prophetic Counsel in the Last Days*
(with Larry E. Dahl and Walter Bowen)

Forgiveness: Christ's Priceless Gift

LDS Beliefs: A Doctrinal Reference
(with Robert L. Millet, Andrew C. Skinner, and Camille Fronk Olson)

A Peculiar Treasure: Old Testament Messages for Our Day

*The Shield of Faith: The Power of Religion in the
Lives of LDS Youth and Young Adults*
(with Bruce Chadwick and Richard J. McClendon)

When You Can't Do It Alone

Talks on CD

Quenching Spiritual Thirst

Strengthened by His Hand

*What's on the Other Side:
What the Gospel Teaches Us about the Spirit World*

WHAT'S ON THE OTHER SIDE?

What the Gospel Teaches Us about the Spirit World

BRENT L. TOP

DESERET
BOOK

SALT LAKE CITY, UTAH

Library of Congress Cataloging-in-Publication Data

Top, Brent L., author.
 What's on the other side? : what the gospel teaches us about the spirit world / Brent L. Top.
  pages cm.
 Includes bibliographical references and index.
 ISBN 978-1-60907-046-5 (hardbound : alk. paper)
 1. Future life—The Church of Jesus Christ of Latter-day Saints. 2. The Church of Jesus Christ of Latter-day Saints—Doctrines. I. Title.
 BX8643.F87T67 2012
 236'.2—dc23   2012003640

Printed in the United States of America
Publishers Printing, Salt Lake City, UT

10   9   8   7   6   5   4   3   2   1

What is this thing that men call death,
This quiet passing in the night?
'Tis not the end, but genesis
Of better worlds and greater light.
O God, touch Thou my aching heart,
And calm my troubled, haunting fears.
Let hope and faith, transcendent, pure,
Give strength and peace beyond my tears.
There is no death, but only change
With recompense for victory won;
The gift of Him who loved all men,
The Son of God, the Holy One.

—PRESIDENT GORDON B. HINCKLEY

CONTENTS

PREFACE

This book is the result of nearly three decades of reading, research, and reflection. I am fascinated with death but not in a morbid or macabre way. I have read every book that I could get my hands on about the subject and am glued to the television whenever there are programs about someone's near-death experience. I am intrigued by the many accounts of people, both Latter-day Saints and those not of our faith, who have been privileged in some manner to glimpse beyond the veil. Death and the notion of life after death are fascinating to me. This fascination, however, does not come because "inquiring minds want to know" or out of some desire for the sensational.

Rather, I am drawn to the doctrine, first and foremost—what the scriptures and prophets teach about death and the spirit world. I look at accounts of near-death experiences within that doctrinal framework. Someone's experience with the spirit world may be *interesting*, but knowledge of the doctrine of the plan of salvation is *imperative*. The doctrine found in the standard works and the teaching of latter-day prophets, seers, and revelators informs us, comforts us, and protects us from deception.

Nearly twenty years ago my wife, Wendy, and I published a book entitled *Beyond Death's Door;* a more recent edition was published as *Glimpses beyond Death's Door.* Our extensive research in preparing that book introduced us to hundreds of accounts of near-death experiences and descriptions of spirit world encounters by Latter-day Saints and by those not of our faith. The more we studied all of these experiences in light of the teachings of the restored gospel, the more convinced we became that Latter-day Saints should keenly understand we do not have a corner on the market when it comes to truth and inspiration. God loves all His children, not just the Latter-day Saints. He answers the prayers of everyone and gives understanding as well. We believe there is a spiritual influence that emanates from "the presence of God to fill the immensity of space" (D&C 88:12). As President Howard W. Hunter stated: "All men share an inheritance of divine light. God operates among his children in all nations, and those who seek God are entitled to further light and knowledge, regardless of their race, nationality, or cultural traditions."[1]

The First Presidency declared in an official statement issued February 15, 1978: "The great religious leaders of the world such as Mohammed, Confucius, and the Reformers, as well as philosophers including Socrates, Plato, and others, received a portion of God's light. Moral truths were given to them by God to enlighten whole nations and to bring a higher level of understanding to individuals." The First Presidency went on to say, "Consistent with these truths, we believe that God has given and will give to all peoples sufficient knowledge to help them on their way to eternal salvation, either in this life or in the life to come."[2]

The doctrines of the Restoration and the enlightenment of the Holy Spirit help us glean truth from many sources. "'Mormonism,'" President Brigham Young declared, "embraces every principle pertaining to life and salvation, for time and eternity. No matter who has it. If the infidel has got truth it belongs to 'Mormonism.' The truth and sound doctrine possessed by the sectarian world, and they have a great deal, all belong to this Church. . . . All that is good, lovely, and praiseworthy belongs to this Church and Kingdom. 'Mormonism' includes all truth."[3] We see this principle manifest in many teachings but particularly with regard to those concerning death and the spirit world. Understanding our own teachings and doctrines on the matter can often be enhanced by the experiences of those of our faith and those not of our faith who have had their own glimpses beyond the veil.

One such individual is Emanuel Swedenborg, an eighteenth-century Swedish scientist, engineer, and religious philosopher who was also a faithful, Bible-believing Christian. He claimed to have been allowed to visit what we would call the spirit world (he called it "heaven and hell") on a frequent and prolonged basis. He described what he saw and learned from these experiences in his classic work, *Heaven and Hell,* which was first published in Latin in 1758 and in English in 1812. Ralph Waldo Emerson characterized Swedenborg as one of the brightest minds in human history—"One of the . . . mastodons of literature" who "is not to be measured by whole colleges of ordinary scholars."[4] Despite his incredible intellect and inspiration, Swedenborg was at a disadvantage in describing what he had seen beyond the veil. He, and others like him who have been blessed with spiritual experiences and visions of eternity, are somewhat limited in their understanding and explanations because they do not possess an understanding and testimony of the gospel of Jesus Christ restored through the Prophet Joseph Smith in this dispensation. As we read their various accounts and descriptions of the spirit world, it is important to keep in mind that the standard works and modern prophets and apostles declare doctrine and provide us the means whereby we can discern truth. In this book, I seek to teach the doctrine from those authoritative sources and use the accounts of others merely to shed some interesting light on the revealed doctrine of death and the spirit world.

When the Prophet Joseph Smith was engaged in the work of translating the Bible, he asked the Lord whether he should translate the Apocrypha. The Lord's response, as found in Doctrine and Covenants 91, gives us some important guidelines as to how to view sources that are outside the established canon or official doctrines of the Church. We can benefit from such apocryphal sources if we recognize that "there are many things contained therein that are true" and "there are many things contained therein that are not true, which are interpolations by the hands of men" (vv. 1–2). As a result, "whoso readeth it, let him understand, for the Spirit manifesteth truth; and whoso is enlightened by the Spirit shall obtain benefit therefrom; and whoso receiveth not by the Spirit, cannot be benefited" (vv. 4–6).

As members of the Church, we are greatly blessed by these

guidelines. It is therefore very important that we measure all accounts of spirit world experiences against the fixed standards of Church doctrine and the witness of the Spirit. The doctrine as declared by prophets and apostles is the spiritually life-sustaining main course; the accounts of near-death experiences are interesting side dishes that, desirable and delicious to the soul, may enhance the whole meal.

Since the publication of *Beyond Death's Door* in 1993, I have written articles, taught classes, and given numerous talks on the postmortal spirit world. In 2008, Deseret Book asked me to give two talks on the subject; they were produced as a CD set entitled *What's on the Other Side?* In the years since, I have received hundreds, if not thousands, of e-mails, letters, and telephone calls from people all over who have listened to those talks. I have been gratified that so many seem to have benefited from my work and found in it comfort and insight. I have been overwhelmed by the many requests that I received for references to the quotations used in the talks. (I can tell when a talk has been rebroadcast on BYUtv by the timing of the increased number of requests.) Many have expressed the desire to have the quotations and references for their own study and to share with others.

So that is how this book came to be. It is essentially those two talks with a little different organization and some additional material. I hope this book will be both informative and inspiring. For me, the doctrine does that; it informs and inspires. May you learn some new things, but most of all, may you feel comfort in times of sadness and loneliness, an assurance of the reality of a glorious life beyond the veil of death when you will be reunited with family and friends, a deeper appreciation for the great plan of happiness, and a stronger desire to live a good life *here and now* so as to have eternal life *then and there.*

I have tried to teach here only those things that are true and in harmony with the restored gospel of Jesus Christ as I understand it. Nonetheless, this book does not represent the official doctrine or position of The Church of Jesus Christ of Latter-day Saints. I alone am responsible for the ideas, insights, and applications presented here. If there are deficiencies or errors, they come strictly from my own deficiencies of understanding, not from my intent. The desire of my heart always is to teach and testify of truth, build faith, and help others find fulfillment in life's journey.

Chapter 1

DYING TO LIVE

W e live to die. In fact, the seeds of death are sown at the same instant life is conceived. That is just part of mortality, in the literal sense of that word. In the eternal scheme of things there can be no life—eternal life—without death. We must die to really live. Death is both fascinating and somewhat frightening in that there is such apprehension about it. Some look forward with great anticipation to death. Others fear the inevitable. Still others are resigned to the fact that we all die and try not to think about it much. Sometimes our fears are expressed not in whether we will die but in speculation about how we will die. "I'm not afraid of death," a friend once said to me. "I'm just afraid of what I will have to go through to get there." Whether we articulate it or not, all of us have an interest in death, whether through fear or simple curiosity or some of each. It is part of human nature. The Prophet Joseph Smith taught that "the Lord in his wisdom has implanted the fear of death in every person that [we] might cling to life and thus accomplish the designs of [our] creator."[1]

Not long ago I visited a dear friend in the hospital shortly before she passed away. She had lived a great life and was certainly prepared to go on. Yet she expressed some degree of apprehension regarding the unknown. She said, "You know, Brent, this is uncharted territory for me." It is uncharted territory for all of us. No matter what our age or circumstances, death is a new experience for each of us. Some look forward to passing to the "other side" where they can be free from pains and sicknesses, toils and troubles, or be reunited with a loved one from whom they have been separated, sometimes for decades. On the other hand, some spend their lives in search of a fountain of youth in hopes they will never die. Still others just ignore it, finding it too unpleasant to think or talk about it much. But ignoring it doesn't eliminate it. Someone once said that life is a terminal illness—no one gets out of it alive. In fact, death is a vital gateway to immortality, an important milestone along the road of eternal progress. For this reason we should learn all we can.

The Prophet Joseph Smith taught: "All men know that they must die. And it is important that we should understand the reasons and causes of our exposure to the vicissitudes of life and of death, and the designs and purposes of God in our coming into the world, our sufferings here, and our departure hence. . . . It is but reasonable to suppose that God would reveal something in reference to the matter, and it is a subject we ought to study more than any other. We ought to study it day and night, for the world is ignorant in reference to their true condition and relation. If we have any claim on our Heavenly

Father for anything, it is for knowledge on this important subject."[2]

Our Heavenly Father has indeed revealed many things to us about the great plan of happiness and the next estate. From the scriptures (both ancient and modern) and the inspired teachings and experiences of prophets, seers, and revelators, we can glimpse beyond the veil of death and gain greater understanding of the role of our death and the conditions of the spirit world. The knowledge gained from the restored gospel is both interesting and inspiring, fascinating and comforting.

While attending the funeral of a friend, President Gordon B. Hinckley penned a poem about death that speaks of this comfort and knowledge. I have loved this poem from the first time I read it, but I was deeply touched by the musical rendition of it that was sung by the Tabernacle Choir at President Hinckley's funeral. The first sentence asks:

> *What is this thing that men call death,*
> *This quiet passing in the night?*[3]

The scriptures answer President Hinckley's question. In Ecclesiastes we read the familiar verse: "Then shall the dust return to the earth as it was: and the spirit shall return unto God who gave it" (Ecclesiastes 12:7). In the Book of Mormon, Alma expanded on this doctrine. He explained that an angel had taught him that at death "the spirits of all men, as soon as they are departed from this mortal body . . . are taken home to that God who gave them life" (Alma 40:11). Many in the world think they cease to exist at death. Many think they sleep until the resurrection. Others speak of life continuing on but don't know exactly how or in what form.

"To the unbeliever [death] is the end of all," President Spencer W. Kimball taught, "associations terminated, relationships ended, memories soon to fade into nothingness. But to those who have knowledge and faith in the promise of the gospel of Jesus Christ, death's meaning is . . . a change of condition into a wider, serener sphere of action; it means the beginning of eternal life."[4] The old phrase, "there is nothing so sure and so final as death" just isn't true. Death is not final at all.

Emanuel Swedenborg, the eighteenth-century Swedish scientist and religious philosopher who was also a faithful, Bible-believing Christian, and many others have given us accounts of their encounters with the spirit world. They tell us that departed spirits in that realm do not use the word *death* in describing their condition. The word that was frequently used was *change*. One person who had a near-death experience said, "It's not death. It's another kind of life." Another described his death as "like going into another dimension. Death is simply an open door."[5]

These people described from their own experiences what we understand through gospel principles taught by prophets and apostles.

We know that death is not the end but only a change, a transition from one condition to another. "Death is not as consummate as many believe," President Boyd K. Packer taught, "it is another graduation. When you come to your commencement from life, you will find a conclusion which is another beginning, this time to have no ending."[6]

Death is the opening of another door in our eternal existence. Without minimizing the sadness that occurs with the loss of a loved one, I like to think of death as walking from one room in the house to another. Doors open and doors close, but we are not really "gone" at all—we're just in a different part of our home. The next sentence in President Hinckley's poem captures it well:

> 'Tis not the end, but genesis
> Of better worlds and greater light.

How blessed we are to have the restored gospel that teaches us of these "better worlds and greater light" as pertaining to what our spirits are like, where the spirit world is, what it is like, and what goes on there. Knowing what death really is (and isn't) and what role it plays in our eternal existence helps us put things into proper perspective. Revelations of the restored gospel teach us, at least conceptually, that death is nothing to be feared if we have lived and loved according to the best we knew.

In our dispensation the Lord declared, "And it shall come to pass that those that die in me shall not taste of death, for it shall be sweet unto them" (D&C 42:46).

President Brigham Young said of death: "We shall turn round and look upon it and think, when we have crossed it, why this is the greatest advantage of my whole existence, for I have passed from a state of sorrow, grief, mourning, woe, misery, pain, anguish and disappointment into a state of existence, where I can enjoy life to the fullest extent as far as that can be done without a body.[7]

The more we come to understand and appreciate the meaning of death in our eternal existence, the more we will appreciate life and use this mortal probation to prepare for "better worlds and greater light." No wonder the Prophet Joseph said this is a subject we ought to study more than any other.

Chapter 2

THE IMMORTAL SPIRIT

M odern revelation teaches us that "the spirit of man [is] in the likeness of his person" (D&C 77:2). In 1909 the First Presidency stated that the body "is only the clothing of the spirit" and that "the spirit of man is in the form of man."[1] We are so familiar with this doctrine that perhaps we take it for granted. Many who are not of our faith, who encounter the spirit world, are surprised that their spirits are in the form of their physical bodies. For example, one woman who had a near-death experience stated that when her spirit left her body she was surprised to find that "I still had hands, and feet, and a body, for I had always regarded the soul as a something without shape and void. . . . [I was surprised] to find, that though I was 'dead' I still had form, [that] was new to me."[2] As this illustrates, there are others not of our faith who also have been blessed with spiritual insights concerning the work-ings of God in general and the concept of life after death in particular. One of these enlightened individuals was Emanuel

Swedenborg, who taught that spirits have human form, even though such a concept was not widely accepted in his day and was even viewed as heretical by most churchmen of his generation. Swedenborg said that he had entered the spirit world on many occasions over many years and described in great detail what he observed and learned there. Concerning the nature of departed spirits (whom he called angels) he wrote: "People in Christendom are in such blind ignorance about angels and spirits that they believe them to be minds without form, or nothing but thoughts, which could not be conceptualized except the way one might conceptualize [a vapor] containing something living. And since they predicate of angels nothing human but thought, they believe they cannot see because they have no eyes, cannot hear because they have no ears, and cannot talk because they have no mouth or tongue. . . .

"On the basis of all my experience, covering to date many years, I can say, I can insist that angels are completely people in form. They do have faces, eyes, ears, chests, arms, hands, and feet. They do see each other, hear each other, and talk with each other. In short, nothing proper to man whatever is missing, except they are not clothed with a material body."[3]

The gospel teaches us that our physical body is indeed the outer shell or tabernacle that houses our immortal spirit. President Boyd K. Packer compared the body and spirit to a hand and glove. The glove covers the hand, but the hand is the real living part. Death is like taking off the glove.[4] President Brigham Young stated: "Take the spirit from the body, and the body is lifeless."[5] This doctrine helps us to understand our feelings when we stand before the open casket bearing the remains of a dear loved one. There is the distinct feeling that the shell before us is "not him" (or her). The body of our loved one is not the "real" person we have loved. The real person is gone—you can feel and see that this is the case.

Free from Physical Defects and Disabilities

The restored gospel teaches us another important truth about the spirit body: it is perfect, not hampered or hindered by physical defects or disabilities. At death, the spirit body is liberated from the adverse effects of aging, disease, or handicaps. Elder Orson Pratt taught: "We, as Latter-day Saints, believe that the spirits that occupy these tabernacles have form and likeness similar to the human tabernacle. Of course there may be deformities existing in connection with the outward tabernacle which do not exist in connection with the spirit that inhabits it. These tabernacles become deformed by accident in various ways, sometimes at birth, but this may not altogether or in any degree deform the spirits that dwell within them."[6]

President Brigham Young said: "I can say with regard to parting with our friends, and going ourselves, that I have been near enough to understand eternity so that I have had to exercise a great deal more faith to desire to live than I ever exercised in my whole life to live. The brightness and glory of the next apartment is inexpressible. It is not encumbered with this clog of dirt we are carrying around here so that when we advance in years we have to be stubbing along and to be careful lest we fall down. . . . But yonder, how different! . . . Here, we are continually troubled with ills and ailments of various kinds, . . . but in the spirit world we are free from all this and enjoy life, glory, and intelligence."[7]

What a comforting doctrine it is to know that physical

limitations will fall away, that disease and sickness in the spirit world are nonexistent and that aging and handicap are nowhere to be found. I find much of modern near-death research fascinating, not because it teaches me anything new about the spirit world, but that it confirms those truths we already know by virtue of the restored gospel. For example, Dr. Elisabeth Kübler-Ross, one of the world's pioneers in hospice care for the terminally ill and the author of *On Death and Dying*, observed that people who had near-death encounters with the spirit world discovered that their spirit bodies were healthy and strong. "Quadriplegics are no longer paralyzed," she wrote, "multiple sclerosis patients who have been in wheelchairs for years say that when they were out of their bodies, they were able to sing and dance."[8] A man who had lost a large portion of his leg in an accident saw, in his near-death experience, the doctors working on his maimed body. He said, "I could feel my [spirit] body, and it was whole. . . . I felt that all of me was there."[9]

Dr. Kenneth Ring, one of the world's foremost near-death experience researchers (who is not of our faith), conducted a groundbreaking study several years ago where people who had been blind from birth—never had any vision whatsoever—who had near-death encounters with the other side reported being able to clearly see. Though they had never seen colors or light or anything before in their lives, they described in detail people, colors, scenes, etc. in the spirit world.[10] Scientists, medical doctors, and psychologists were left scratching their heads to explain this. But to us, it makes perfect sense. Of course they would see because their spirit eyes can see, even if their physical eyes can't. Because of what the restored gospel teaches us about spirits and the spirit world we are not surprised as some who have had near-death experiences and those who research the phenomenon are to hear of spirits seeing, feeling, hearing, thinking, smelling, walking, running, and jumping.

Enhanced Capacities of the Spirit Body

In fact, from the restored gospel we learn that the powers and capacities of the spirit body surpass even those of physical bodies in the natural world when it comes to communication and feelings, movement and travel, and learning and comprehension. From the Doctrine and Covenants we learn that "all spirit is matter, but it is more fine or pure, and can only be discerned by purer eyes" (D&C 131:7). The refined, pure nature of spirit matter affects how the spirit moves about, communicates, learns, and comprehends. I'm not a physicist and I don't profess to understand how it all works, but I find the scriptural statements about matter and the statements of early prophets and apostles about spirit capacities extraordinarily fascinating.

Movement and Travel

The nature and makeup of the spirit body are a factor in its ability to move in a way that we might characterize as supernatural. Elder Parley P. Pratt taught that the "refined particles" of spirit allow it to "penetrate amid the other elements with greater ease, and meet with less resistance from the air or other substances, than would the more gross elements. Hence its speed, or superior powers of motion."[11] One of the most remarkable ways whereby spirits demonstrate "superior powers of motion" can be seen in these amazing statements by Brigham Young: "As quickly as the spirit is unlocked from this house of clay, it is free to travel with lightning speed to any planet, or fixed star, or to the uttermost part of the earth, or to the depths of the sea, according to the will of Him who dictates."[12] And, "[spirits] move with ease and like lightning. If we want to visit Jerusalem, or this, that, or the other place—and I presume we will be permitted if we desire—there we are, looking at its streets. If we want to behold Jerusalem as it was in the days of the Savior; or if we want to see the Garden of Eden as it was when created, there we are, and we see it as it existed spiritually, for it was created first spiritually and then temporally, and spiritually it still remains. And when there we may behold the earth as at the dawn of creation, or we may visit any city we please that exists upon its surface. If we wish to understand how they are living here on these western islands, or in China, we are there; in fact, we are like the light of the morning, or, I will not say the electric fluid, but its operations on the wires. God has revealed some little things with regard to His movements and power, and the operation and motion of the lightning furnish a fine illustration of the ability and power of the Almighty. . . . When we pass into the spirit world we shall possess a measure of this power."[13]

I don't know how time travel works, but I do know that in the spirit world and to God, time and space are different than here on earth. As Elder Neal A. Maxwell declared: "When the veil which now encloses us is no more, time will also be no more (D&C 84:100). Even now, time is clearly not our natural dimension. Thus it is that we are never really at home in time. . . . Time, as much as any one thing, whispers to us that we are strangers here."[14]

Communication

The Lord revealed to the Prophet Joseph Smith that the means whereby God communicates with man is through the mind and in the heart (see D&C 8:2). He later taught that divine messages from the eternal realm come to us "independent of affinity of this mortal tabernacle, but are revealed to our spirits precisely as though we had no bodies at all."[15] The spirit of revelation is the divine means of communication not only here in mortality, but also in the next life. Such divine communication transcends words and language. Elder Orson Pratt taught: "How do you suppose that spirits after they leave these bodies, communicate one with another? Do they communicate their ideas by the actual vibrations of the atmosphere the same as we do? I think not. I think if we could be made acquainted with the kind of language by which spirits converse with spirits, we would find that they . . . have undoubtedly a more refined system among them of communicating their ideas. This system will be so constructed that they can, not only communicate at the same moment upon one subject, as we have to do by making sounds in the atmosphere, but communicate vast numbers of ideas, all at the same time, on a great variety of subjects; and the mind will be capable of perceiving them. . . . If the mind has such faculty as this, then there must necessarily be a language adapted to such a capacity of the mind."

Elder Pratt goes on to explain how that divine communication between spirits occurs: "Well inquires one, 'Can you imagine up any such system, or language in this world?' I can imagine up one, but it cannot be made practicable here, from the fact that the mind of man is unable to use it. For instance, the Book of Mormon tells us, that the angels speak by the power of the Holy Ghost, and man when under the influence of it, speaks the language of angels. Why does he speak in this language? Because the Holy Ghost suggests the ideas which he speaks; and it gives him utterance to convey them to the people. . . . Suppose, instead of having arbitrary sounds, such as we have here, to communicate these ideas, that the Holy Ghost itself, through a certain process and power should enable him to unfold that knowledge to another spirit, all in an instant."[16]

With such perfect communication in that realm, no wonder those who come back from a spirit world encounter have difficulty putting into human words what they learned, what they heard, what they felt, and what they experienced. Emanuel Swedenborg said of that spirit world communication:

"Their speech is so full of wisdom that they with a single word can express things that men could not compass in a thousand words. Then, too, their thought-concepts embrace things such as men cannot grasp, let alone verbalize. Consequently, the sounds and sights of heaven are called inexpressible, and such as ear simply has not yet heard, nor eye seen."[17]

Ability to Learn, Comprehend, and Remember

Another important capacity of the spirit body is the ability to learn and comprehend. We know that the spirit world is a place of learning. The gospel teaches us that the most important learning is acquired though spiritual means. "I shall not cease learning while I live, nor when I arrive in the spirit-world," President Brigham Young observed, "but shall there learn with greater facility."[18] Likewise, Elder Orson Pratt taught that our ability to absorb, comprehend, and remember information is "greatly enlarged." He said: "We shall learn many more things there; we need not suppose our five senses connect us with all the things of heaven, and earth, and eternity, and space; we need not think that we are conversant with all the elements of nature, through the medium of the senses God has given us here. Suppose He should give us a sixth sense, a seventh, an eighth, a ninth, or a fiftieth. All these different senses would convey to us new ideas, as much so as the senses of tasting, smelling, or seeing communicate different ideas from that of hearing."[19] He also asked, "How long a time would it take a man in the next world, if he had to gain knowledge as we do here, to find out the simplest things in nature? He might reason, and reason for thousands of years, and then hardly have got started. But when this Spirit of God, this great telescope that is used in the celestial heavens, is given to man, and he, through the aid of it, gazes upon eternal things, what does he behold? Not one object at a time, but a vast multitude of objects rush before his vision, and are present before his mind, filling him in a moment with the knowledge of worlds more numerous than the sands of the sea shore. Will he be able to bear it? Yes, his mind is strengthened. . . . It is this tabernacle, in its present condition, that prevents us from a more enlarged understanding. . . .

"I believe we shall be freed, in the next world, in a great measure, from these narrow, contracted methods of thinking. Instead of thinking in one channel, and following up one certain course of reasoning to find a certain truth, knowledge will rush in from all quarters; it will come in like the light which flows from the sun, penetrating every part, informing the spirit, and giving understanding concerning ten thousand things at the same time; and the mind will be capable of receiving and retaining all."[20]

I look forward to that enhanced capacity to learn. In addition, there is one capacity of spirit learning that appeals to me: not only will I learn faster and completely, but I will actually remember it! Elder Pratt added: "We read or learn a thing by observation yesterday, and to-day or to-morrow it is gone. . . . Some of the knowledge we receive here at one time becomes so completely obliterated, through the weakness of [our physical bodies], that we cannot call it to mind, no association of ideas will again suggest it to our minds; it is gone, erased, eradicated from the tablet of our memories. . . . [Why?] because there is imperfection in the organization of the flesh and bones, and in things pertaining to the tabernacle; it is this that erases from our memory many things that would be useful. . . . It is not so with the spirit when it is released from this tabernacle. . . . Wait until these mortal bodies are laid in the tomb . . . then is the time we shall have the most vivid knowledge [and memory]."[21]

Such descriptions of the learning that takes place in the spirit world illustrate perfectly what the Prophet Joseph Smith was referring to when he declared: "Could you gaze into heaven five minutes, you would know more than you would by reading all that ever was written on the subject."[22]

"Enveloped in Flaming Fire"

In a funeral sermon for James Adams delivered in Nauvoo on 9 October 1843, the Prophet Joseph Smith stated that at death "the spirits of the just are exalted to a greater and more glorious work; hence they are blessed in their departure to the world of spirits. *Enveloped in flaming fire,* they are not far from us."[23] There are two important concepts conveyed in that statement. First, the phrase "enveloped in flaming fire": In the scriptures, fire is used to symbolize God's power and glory. Clearly, the Prophet is teaching us that our righteous loved ones enter into the spirit world only to be "clothed," as it were, with fire, with greater power and the glory of God. We are not fully clothed in God's glory until after a glorious resurrection, but as seen in the teachings of the prophets cited in this chapter, at death our spiritual capacities are greatly enhanced—"enveloped in flaming fire" with a greater degree of God's power than we knew in mortality. We have examined in this chapter what the immortal spirit is like after death. In the next chapter we will explore the second important concept. We will see more clearly what the Prophet meant when he said of our deceased loved ones: "they are not far from us."

Chapter 3

THE SPIRIT WORLD

We have discussed the nature of our spirits: what they are like and what they can do. Now let us address the issue of the spirit world, the habitation of our immortal spirits when they leave our bodies at death: where it is and what it is like.

Where Is the Spirit World?

People often think of the spirit world (or "heaven") being up in the sky or somewhere in outer space. Because of the restoration of the gospel we know that is not the case. President Brigham Young said: "Where is the spirit world? It is right here. Do the good and evil spirits go together? Yes, they do. . . . Do they go to the sun [or some other planet]? No. Do they go beyond the boundaries of this organized earth? No, they do not. They are brought forth upon this earth, for the express purpose of inhabiting it to all eternity."[1] How is it that the spirit world can be right here on this earth? Is it a different dimension? Elder Parley P. Pratt perhaps explained it best: "The earth and other planets of a like sphere, have their inward or spiritual spheres, as well as their outward, or temporal. The one is peopled by temporal tabernacles, and the other by spirits. A veil is drawn between the one sphere and the other, whereby all the objects in the spiritual sphere are rendered invisible to those in the temporal."[2]

Many people not of our faith and who had never been taught regarding the location of the world of spirits have had remarkable experiences that confirm this doctrine. One young girl who was dying, for whom the veil had become very thin, made a comment to her family of the nearness of the spirit world. Two days before she died, her Sunday School teacher came to see her and comfort her. As he was leaving, he said, "'Well, Daisy; you will soon be over the dark river,' obviously referring to her imminent death. Daisy appeared puzzled by the reference. 'There is no river,' she replied, 'there is no curtain, there is not even a line that separates this life from the other life.'"[3] Many others who passed into the spirit world and later returned to this life spoke of being able to see into the mortal world while they were dead, including seeing their own deceased bodies, but that the physical beings could not see or hear them. Dr. Maurice Rawlings observed from his own experience that people on earth are "blinded," as it were, to "this spiritual world" that surrounds "our present life."[4]

One of my favorite accounts comes from the Reverend Norman Vincent Peale. Upon receiving word that his mother had died, he went into the church sanctuary to be alone to think, pray, and grieve the loss of his beloved mother. She had often told him that whenever he went to the pulpit to preach she would be with him. He hoped she would be with him now.

He said: "I sat for quite a while. Then, leaving the pulpit, I went into my office, stood in front of my desk, and put my hand on a Bible my mother had given me when I became [a] minister . . . some 17 years earlier. At that moment, I felt two strong hands, cupped together, as light as a feather, on the back of my head. And I had the distinct impression of her person indicating to me that it was all right, and that she was happy, and to grieve no more.

"As a product of a scientific theological education, I had some trouble with this, even though I was a son longing for his departed mother. But then I began to read all the literature in this field, and discovered that something of similar nature has happened to thousands of people.

"That leads me to the conclusion that this other world is not way off in the sky someplace, but that it is superimposed upon the world in which we live. That other world is simply on a higher, or, at least, a different frequency than we on earth occupy. And the line of demarcation becomes, under certain circumstances, so thin that there can be a vibration, or the sense of a presence, so that we know those whom we have loved and lost are not far from us."[5]

Dr. Peale's experience and those of many others confirm what prophets have taught us, including President Joseph F. Smith, who declared: "I believe we move and have our being in the presence of heavenly messengers and of heavenly beings. We are not separate from them. . . . And therefore, I claim that we live in their presence, they see us, they are solicitous for our welfare, they love us now more than ever."[6]

What Is the Spirit World Like?

The Lord revealed to the Prophet Joseph Smith in Doctrine and Covenants 77:2 that "that which is temporal [is] in the likeness of that which is spiritual." From that we can assume that the spirit world is much like this world. President Brigham Young, who himself had seen the spirit world on more than one occasion, declared: "When you are in the spirit world, everything there will appear as natural as things now do. Spirits will be familiar with spirits in the spirit world—will converse, behold, and exercise every variety of communication one with another as familiarly and naturally as while here in tabernacles. There, as here, all things will be natural, and you will understand them as you now understand natural things."[7]

While the scriptures and prophets teach us that the spirit world will appear natural to us and be much like this world, I think we can assume that it will be what I call "natural-plus," or as Joseph Smith taught, "coupled with eternal glory, which glory we do not now enjoy" (D&C 130:2). In some ways we might compare it to the difference between the quality of early over-the-air analog television broadcasts and today's high-definition digital broadcasts.

Jedediah M. Grant, counselor to Brigham Young and father to President Heber J. Grant, saw the spirit world shortly before his death and recounted what he saw to President Heber C. Kimball: "'Brother Heber, I have been into the spirit world two nights in succession, and, of all the dreads that ever came across me, the worst was to have to again return to my body, though I had to do it. . . .'

"He also spoke of the buildings he saw there, remarking that the Lord gave Solomon wisdom and poured gold and silver into his hands that he might display his skill and ability, and said that the temple erected by Solomon was much inferior to the most ordinary buildings he saw in the spirit world.

"In regards to gardens, says brother Grant, 'I have seen good gardens on this earth, but I never saw any to compare with those that were there. I saw flowers of numerous kinds, and some with fifty to a hundred different colored flowers growing upon one stalk.' We have many kinds of flowers on the earth, and I suppose those very articles came from heaven, or they would not be here. . . .

"After speaking of the gardens and the beauty of every thing there, brother Grant said that he felt extremely sorrowful at having to leave so beautiful a place and come back to earth, for he looked upon his body with loathing, but was obliged to enter it again."[8]

President Grant's experience is strikingly similar to many of the experiences and descriptions given by others, including Brigham Young. No wonder Brigham said that it took far greater faith than he had ever before exercised for him to desire to continue to live in mortality. Numerous others, both Latter-day Saints and those not of our faith, have left descriptions of the remarkable beauty and glory of the next estate. There is an account of an early twentieth-century visit to the spirit world by Heber Q. Hale, an LDS stake president from Boise, Idaho, that is quite well known in the Church. Though it has never been officially endorsed by the Church, it has been published in a variety of sources. President Hale's description corresponds with others regarding the brilliant light and colors of the spirit world. He said, "The vegetation and landscape was beautiful beyond description, like a rainbow, not all green, but gold with various shades of pink, orange, and lavender. . . . [There were] spacious stretches of flowers, grasses, and shrubbery, all of a golden hue."⁹ A man not of our faith who, through a near-death experience, encountered the spirit world described it this way: "I was in a garden. All the colors were intense. The grass was a deep vibrant green, flowers were radiant reds, yellows, and blues, and birds of all beauty fluttered in the bushes. Everything was lit by a shadowless brilliance that was all-pervading.

"This light did not cast a shadow, which I realized when I cupped my hands tightly together and the palm side was just as light as the back side. There were no sounds of motors or discord or commotions. No sound but the songs of birds and the sounds (yes, the 'sounds') of flowers blooming."¹⁰

There is another condition of the spirit world mentioned in these accounts that I find fascinating and in harmony with the teachings of the gospel, and that is the role of music. The Lord declared in our dispensation that "my soul delighteth in the song of the heart; yea, the song of the righteous is a prayer unto me" (D&C 25:12). We know the power that music has on this side of the veil. Music is one of the most important ways in which we commune with God. Certainly music would play a similar role in the spirit world. Many near-death experiences and accounts from others who have glimpsed into the spirit world in some way have commented on music in that realm. One said: "My ears were filled with a music so beautiful no composer could ever duplicate it. . . . It was soothing, gentle, and warm and seemed to come from a source deep within me."¹¹

Another observed: "There was tremendous sound, too. It was as if all the great orchestras in the world were playing at once; no special melody, and very loud, powerful but somehow soothing. It was a rushing, moving sound, unlike anything I could remember, but familiar, just on the edge of my memory."[12]

And another: "I saw many thousand spirits clothed in white, and singing heavenly music—the sweetest song I have ever heard."[13]

After reading these descriptions, a passage from the Book of Mormon jumped out at me and took on new significance. It is the account of Alma the Younger's experience. After being released from the awful pains of hell, he said he had seen "numberless concourses of angels, in the attitude of singing and praising their God; yea, and my soul did long to be there" (Alma 36:22). President Brigham Young declared: "There is no music in hell, for all good music belongs to heaven."[14]

In addition to beauty, brilliant colors, serenity and peace, and soothing music, prophets and others have also described buildings that put the magnificent temple of Solomon to shame. Now, that raises an important question: What are the buildings in the spirit world made of? To which I jokingly answer, "Spirit bricks!" I don't know what building materials are used in the spirit world, but we do know that spirit is element, is matter: "That which is temporal in the likeness of — that which is spiritual" (D&C 77:2). Brigham Young said that it will appear very natural to us; dwelling on clouds doesn't seem very natural. Emanuel Swedenborg, almost a hundred years before the Restoration, described what he had seen in his encounter with the spirit world: "Since [spirits] are people, living together as people on earth do, they have clothes, houses, and many similar things. But there is this difference, that since [spirits] are in a more perfect state, everything they have is more perfect."[15]

Swedenborg goes on to describe it this way: "Their dwellings are just like the dwellings on earth which we call homes, except that they are more beautiful. They have rooms, suites, and bedrooms, all in abundance. They have courtyards, and [are] surrounded by gardens, flowerbeds, and lawns. . . .

"I have seen palaces in heaven so noble as to defy description. . . . Inside, . . . the rooms were decorated with accessories such that words and arts fail to describe them.

"Outside, . . . there were parks where everything likewise glowed, with here and there leaves gleaming like silver and fruit like gold. The flowers in their plots formed virtual rainbows."[16]

It is important to note that Swedenborg was not a prophet, seer, and revelator and he certainly doesn't declare doctrine for us, but it is interesting to note the similarities of his descriptions to those given by Joseph Smith, Brigham Young, Jedediah Grant, Heber C. Kimball, Parley and Orson Pratt, and Joseph F. Smith.

"The Same Sociality"

In Doctrine and Covenants 130 we read that "that same sociality which exists among us here will exist among us there, *only it will be coupled with eternal glory,* which glory we do not now enjoy" (D&C 130:2; emphasis added). What does that mean? What is sociality? It seems to indicate that the same kinds of social interactions and feelings that we enjoy here in this life will continue in that realm, only to a greater and more glorious degree. The Prophet Joseph Smith and Brigham Young both assured the Saints that our interaction with friends and loved ones after this life will be an eternal extension of our joyous association with them here on earth. Brigham Young taught that "spirits will be familiar with spirits in the spirit world—will converse, behold, and exercise every variety of communication with one another as familiarly and naturally as while here in tabernacles."[17] I've often wondered, in light of this "same sociality" doctrine, What do spirits talk about? Certainly the great work of the Lord, but what else? Emanuel Swedenborg gave an interesting answer to the question, "What do spirits talk about?" He said: "[Spirits] talk with each other just the way people in the world do, and they talk of various things—household [family] matters, political matters, issues of moral life and issues of spiritual life, for example. There is no noticeable difference, except that they talk with each other more intelligently than men do, since they talk more profoundly, from thought."[18]

Don't you find it interesting that Swedenborg included political matters in his list? I hope the political discussions on the other side are more civil than those on this side. If our political discussions in the spirit world are even a little bit like some of the discussions we have had in our family circles, there will be far more heat generated than light!

I also hope that "same sociality" also means fun and laughter as well as rejoicing and praising. My mortal "sociality" involves joking and teasing and a lot of laughing and enthusiastic cheering for my favorite sports teams. Good humor brings us pleasure and happiness in this life. I hope that continues on the other side. In fact, I found several accounts of people who had near-death experiences who reported that humor exists and abounds in the spirit world. Let me share some with you.

Dr. George Ritchie, whose spirit world encounter is recorded in the bestselling book *Return from Tomorrow,* spoke of the being that met him and guided him through the spirit world. He said: "If I'd suspected before that there was mirth in the Presence beside me, now I was sure of it: the [Being of Light] seemed to vibrate and shimmer with a kind of holy laughter—not at me and my silliness, not a mocking laughter, but a mirth that seemed to say that in spite of all error and tragedy, joy was more lasting still."[19]

Another person described the people in the spirit world as being "fun . . . to be with" and having "a sense of humor, too—definitely!"[20] Another said that his two spirit companions had "a terrific sense of humor. They made jokes about different things as we were walking and made it very light."[21] I like that! It is comforting to know that we will still be able to laugh in the life after death. It will not be all solemnity and seriousness. We shouldn't be surprised by the fact that joyful humor is also part of the light and love that pervade the afterlife. We can attest to their uplifting power here on earth. Think of people that we love and admire, people who are close to the Lord and deeply committed to the gospel, prophets and apostles and others who love to laugh and enjoy using humor to lift and bring joy to others. I certainly believe that humor and laughter and fun are important aspects of that "same sociality" that exists there . . . maybe I will fit in after all!

A House of Order

The Lord said in the Doctrine and Covenants, "Behold, mine house is a house of order, . . . and not a house of confusion" (D&C 132:8). Order and organization are certainly important characteristics in the spirit-world paradise. "Righteous spirits are close by us," President Ezra Taft Benson taught. "They are organized according to priesthood order in family organizations as we are here; only there they exist in a more perfect order. This was revealed to the Prophet Joseph."[22] This principle was clearly manifest in an important vision that Brigham Young had as the Saints were crossing the plains. He stated that the Prophet Joseph came to him and instructed him and gave counsel to be shared with the Saints. The Prophet told Brigham to "be sure to tell the people to keep the Spirit of the Lord; and if they will, they will find themselves just as they were organized by our Father in Heaven before they came into the world. Our Father in Heaven organized the human family, but they are all disorganized in great confusion."[23] President Jedediah M. Grant also marveled at this extensive order and organization in the spirit world: "But O, . . . the order and government that were there! When in the spirit world, I saw the order of righteous men and women; beheld them organized in their several grades, and there appeared to be no obstruction to my vision; I could see every man and woman in their grade and order. I looked to see whether there was any disorder there, but there was none. . . . The people [I] there saw were organized in family capacities; and when [I] looked at them [I] saw grade after grade, and all were organized and in perfect harmony."[24]

The order and organization of the spirit world was also noted by President Heber Q. Hale. He said: "The people I met there I did not think of as spirits, but as men and women— self-thinking, self-acting individuals, going about important business in a most orderly manner. There was perfect order, and everyone had something to do and seemed to be about their business."[25]

I like the phrases "going about important business in a most orderly manner" and "everyone had something to do." As Swedenborg observed, "Clearly then, the Lord's kingdom is a kingdom of useful activities."[26] Just as we have responsibilities here in this life, we will have responsibilities and work to do there. In fact, many of those who have glimpsed beyond the veil speak of the "busy nature" of the afterlife. As one person not of our faith who had a near-death experience said: "It's a place of intense light, a place of intense activity, more like a bustling city than a lonely country scene, nothing like floating on clouds or [playing] harps or anything of that sort."[27] A woman who had lost a husband and two children saw them in the spirit world and said, "They aren't dead. They are all alive, busy and waiting for me."[28]

Alma taught that, for the righteous, the spirit world will be a paradise, "a state of rest, a state of peace, where they shall rest from all their troubles and from all care, and sorrow" (Alma 40:12). I have often wondered how we can be in a place of rest and yet be busy and deeply involved in intense activity. It reminds me of an account that one of my colleagues shared with me. His aged mother-in-law who had been widowed for decades saw into the spirit world shortly before her passing. She told the family that she had seen departed family members, including her beloved husband. "Well, doesn't that make you want to go join them?" a daughter asked her. To which she responded, "Oh, no. They were so busy. It made me tired watching them."

The spirit world is indeed a place of peace and rest for

the righteous: rest from earthly concerns, freedom from mortal aches and pains and vexing problems, and peace in knowing that our probation is ended and that we have endured faithfully. However, "a state of rest" does not mean lounging about with nothing to do. It is peaceful and spiritually restful to be engaged in the work of the Lord. That is the greatest work to be done on the other side of the veil.

Chapter 4

MINISTERS OF THE GOSPEL

President Wilford Woodruff learned firsthand why people on the other side are so busy. He told of a vision he received of the spirit world in which he spoke with the Prophet Joseph Smith. President Woodruff said: "I saw him at the door of the temple in heaven. He came to me and spoke to me. He said he could not stop to talk with me because he was in a hurry. The next man I met was Father Smith [Joseph, Sr.]; he could not talk with me because he was in a hurry. I met [a] half dozen brethren who held high positions on earth, and none of them could stop to talk with me because they were in a hurry. I was much astonished. By and by I saw the Prophet again and I got the privilege of asking him a question.

"'Now,' said I, 'I want to know why you are in a hurry. I have been in a hurry all my life; but I expected my hurry would be over when I got into the kingdom of heaven, if I ever did.'

"Joseph said: 'I will tell you, Brother Woodruff. Every

dispensation that has had the priesthood on the earth and has gone into the celestial kingdom has had a certain amount of work to do to prepare to go to earth with the Savior when he goes to reign on the earth. Each dispensation has had ample time to do this work. We have not. We are the last dispensation, and so much work has to be done, and we need to be in a hurry to accomplish it.'"[1]

Hurry is the operative word. Urgency would describe the work on the other side of the veil. We know what that work is in which the righteous spirits are so busily engaged. It is the preaching of the gospel of Jesus Christ, as Isaiah described it, "[proclaiming] liberty to the captives, and the opening of the prison to them that are bound" (Isaiah 61:1).

In one of the great revelations of the Restoration, President Joseph F. Smith saw in vision the opening of this vital work in the world of the spirits. On 3 October 1918, President Smith sat in his room pondering the scriptures when, as he said, "the eyes of my understanding were opened, and the Spirit of the Lord rested upon me, and I saw the hosts of the dead, both small and great" (D&C 138:1, 11). Of the righteous spirits, President Smith said: "I beheld that they were filled with joy and gladness, and were rejoicing together because the day of their deliverance was at hand.

"They were assembled awaiting the advent of the Son of God into the spirit world, to declare their redemption from the bands of death. . . . While this vast multitude waited and conversed, rejoicing in the hour of their deliverance from the chains of death, the Son of God appeared, declaring liberty to the captives who had been faithful; and there he preached to them the everlasting gospel, the doctrine of the resurrection and the redemption of mankind from the fall, and from individual sins on conditions of repentance. But unto the wicked he did not go, and among the ungodly and the unrepentant who had defiled themselves while in the flesh, his voice was not raised; neither did the rebellious who rejected the testimonies and the warnings of the ancient prophets behold his presence, nor look upon his face. Where these were, darkness reigned, but among the righteous there was peace" (D&C 138:15–16, 18–22).

After seeing in vision the Savior's ministry among the righteous in the spirit world, President Smith wondered how the gospel would go forth to all the other spirits in that realm. He then saw how the Lord "organized his forces and appointed messengers, clothed with power and authority, and commissioned them to go forth and carry the light of the gospel to them that were in darkness, even to all the spirits of men; and thus was the gospel preached to the dead" (D&C 138:28, 30).

That is the urgent work in which all faithful spirits will find themselves engaged when they depart this life and enter into the world of the spirits. There is no doubt in my mind that the work of the Lord in the spirit world follows much the same pattern as the work of the Lord does in this life—leading, teaching, fellowshipping, strengthening—all under the direction of the priesthood. As President Wilford Woodruff declared: "The same priesthood exists on the other side of the veil. Every man who is faithful is in his quorum there. When a man dies and his body is laid in the tomb, he does not lose his position. The Prophet Joseph Smith held the keys of this dispensation on this side of the veil, and he will hold them throughout the ages of eternity. He went into the spirit world to unlock the prison doors and to preach the gospel to the millions of spirits who are in darkness, and every apostle, every seventy [every high priest], every elder, etc., who has died in the faith, as soon as he passes to the other side of the veil, enters into the work of the ministry, and there is a thousand times more to preach there than there is here."[2]

President Woodruff highlights the work in the spirit world done by priesthood holders. But we know that much of the Lord's work on this side of the veil is also done by faithful sisters. And it is the same on the other side. President Joseph F. Smith observed: "Among all these millions of spirits that have lived on earth and have passed away, from generation to generation, since the beginning of the world, without the knowledge of the gospel—among them you count that at least one-half are women. Who is going to preach the gospel to the women? Who is going to carry the testimony of Jesus Christ to the hearts of the women who have passed away without a knowledge of the gospel? Well, to my mind, it is a simple thing. . . . [Faithful sisters] will be fully authorized and empowered to preach the gospel and minister to the women while the elders and prophets are preaching it to the men. *The things we experience here are typical of the things of God and the life beyond us.*"[3]

Because of the importance and urgency of the work of the Lord in the spirit world, there are times when faithful men and women are called to that work before we may think that they are ready to die. Similar to Church callings here in mortality, deaths are sometimes unexpected and come at what we may think are inopportune times. Elder Neal A. Maxwell gave an insightful observation of this fact. He said: "On the other side of the veil, there are perhaps seventy billion people. They need the same gospel, and releases occur here to aid the Lord's work there. Each release of a righteous individual from this life is also a call to new labors. Those who have true hope understand this. Therefore, though we miss the departed righteous so much here, hundreds may feel their touch there. One day, those hundreds will thank the bereaved for gracefully forgoing the extended association with choice individuals here, in order that they could help hundreds there. In God's ecology, talent and love are never wasted. . . . A mortal life may need to be 'shortened' by twenty years as we might view—but if so, it may be done in order for special services to be rendered by that individual in the spirit world, services that will benefit thousands of new neighbors."[4]

Certainly, Elder Maxwell was one of those. He died before we were ready to let him go and now continues to serve and bless others on the other side of the veil. We know many others whose labors continue, though they have transferred to a different mission field. Whether one dies at nine days or ninety-nine years, their loved ones who are left behind feel the loss and wish they could have had more time together. It is comforting, however, to know that they will be engaged in meaningful service to others: bringing souls to Christ and helping them partake of the fulness of His gospel. It is not unlike what we experience in mortality when parents send a young son or daughter out as full-time missionaries. There are tears shed and sadness felt at the temporary separation. There is anxious waiting for any and every message concerning their work and well-being. Tears of sadness are replaced by tears of joy when we understand how much our missionary is loved by those he or she serves. There is incredible fulfillment in learning how that service has blessed others, transformed lives, and led to temple ordinances that open the door for a fulness of joy in eternity. The temporary separation accompanied by deep missing of our loved one is all worth it. When the mission is fulfilled as the Lord intended, the reunion with loved ones could not be sweeter. So it is and so it will be with our missionaries who now labor in the world of spirits.

Though the work of the Lord will be much the same on that side of the veil, the success attending it will be much greater there than here. That is another profound and comforting thought. President Lorenzo Snow said: "I believe, strongly too, that when the Gospel is preached to the spirits in prison, the success attending that preaching will be far greater than that attending the preaching of our Elders in this life. I believe there will be very few indeed of those spirits who will not gladly receive the Gospel when it is carried to them. The circumstances there will be a thousand times more favorable."5 Can you imagine the happiness in the hearts of both spirit world "missionaries" and their "converts" when that kind of success accompanies the work?

As it is here in the mortal world, not everyone will embrace the gospel message and choose the path of righteousness. One of the interesting things about Joseph F. Smith's vision of the Savior's ministry in the spirit world is the noticeable lack of what we would characterize as wicked spirits and those who had not previously embraced the gospel. We know, as Brigham Young taught, that all go to the same spirit world—righteous, wicked, and everyone in between. On one occasion he taught: "If we go back to our mother country [or the states we have come from], we there find the righteous, and we there find the wicked; if we go to California, we there find the righteous and the wicked, all dwelling together; and when we go beyond this vail, and leave our bodies which were taken from mother earth, and which must return; our spirits will pass beyond the vail; we go where both Saints and sinners go: they all go to one place."[6]

Even though the spirit world is the same place for all, there appears to be some sort of segregation of spirits. It may be something of a self-segregation, according to those things we love and those principles that have guided our lives. That helps to explain why Joseph F. Smith did not see wicked spirits among the righteous when the Savior ministered in the spirit world. The righteous chose to be in holy places learning of holy things. I like to call this principle the "Law of Spiritual Attraction." In Doctrine and Covenants 88:40 we read, "For intelligence cleaveth unto intelligence; wisdom receiveth wisdom; truth embraceth truth; virtue loveth virtue; light cleaveth unto light; mercy hath compassion on mercy and claimeth her own."

We tend to associate with those we feel comfortable around. It probably works much the same way on the other side of the veil. The result of that is, as Parley P. Pratt said, that "there are many places and degrees in that world."[7] President George Q. Cannon, who served as a counselor in the First Presidency to four Church presidents—Brigham Young, John Taylor, Wilford Woodruff, and Lorenzo Snow—said: "There will be just as much distinction between spirits there as you find between spirits here. Those who have made good use of their opportunities here will have the benefit of their diligence and faithfulness there. Those who have been careless and indifferent . . . will find themselves lacking there."[8] It appears that, to a large extent, the circumstances and conditions in the spirit world are of our own making and the division is largely self-selected. Heber Q. Hale, in his vision of the spirit world, saw that "the inhabitants of the spirit world are [congregated] according to how they lived and their obedience to the Father's will. Particularly, I observed that the wicked and unrepentant are confined to a certain district by themselves, the confines of which are definitely determined and impassable . . . until the person himself has changed."⁹ This seems to confirm what the Prophet Joseph taught when he declared that the "wicked spirits have their bounds, limits, and laws by which they are governed or controlled."¹⁰ It's not necessary to have borders or barriers, chains, locks, or prison cells. As on earth, righteousness yields greater freedom and enjoyment. Wickedness yields spiritual captivity and misery as confining as actual chains. Liberation and light comes in the spirit world, as it does here, by learning, accepting, and living the principles and ordinances of the gospel.

Chapter 5

WELCOME HOME

We often speak of death as "going home." In funeral sermons or obituaries the phrase "called home" or "returned home" is used to refer to the deceased's state. Alma used that term in describing death in the Book of Mormon (see Alma 40:11). Because of the restoration of the gospel, we know that we are literally sons and daughters of God, the offspring of heavenly parents. We lived with them in a spirit realm before we came to earth. In some significant way, the spirit world will have a feeling of home. It is not the final stop in our eternal journey, for we will still be resurrected and enter into an eternal kingdom of glory. Though there will still be some veil of forgetfulness, a feeling of familiarity with people and principles will prevail—at least for some. President Brigham Young said that when we get to the other side, "[we will] see that [we] had formerly lived there for ages . . . and [we] had previously been acquainted with every nook and corner, with the palaces, walks, and gardens," and that we will say, "O my Father, my Father, I am here again."[1]

This feeling of familiarity is illustrated in several accounts of those who parted the veil in some way and have glimpsed the spirit world. Some were LDS; most were not. A young teen-age girl said that her first reaction was to say "homey home." When she described this feeling to her family after her brush with death, they told her that that is what she used to say as a toddler as they would approach their neighborhood when they had been away from home. She said, "I would stand in the seat and say . . . homey home, homey home. [That is exactly how I felt.] . . . I was back home absolutely."[2] Another person said: "[It was a] homecoming. . . . I have never really verbalized that before. It was really like a homecoming."[3] Another person that had a near-death experience as a victim of an attempted murder described the feeling this way, "Everything that oc-curred to me while I was in this state of conscious[ness] was vastly beyond anything I had ever experienced and *yet at the same time it was familiar—as if I had always known of its exis-tence*."[4] A final example is from a person who had briefly been in the spirit world after being involved in a serious accident and who declared, "I felt as if I was going back somewhere I belonged. There were people all around who I sensed were lov-ing friends."[5] Being surrounded by loving friends and family is certainly an apt description of home.

Home is a word with sacred meaning both in this life and in the life to come. A few years ago, I got a glimpse of the meaning of that word and how it applies to our "returning home" when we die. After serving as a mission president for three years, my wife, Wendy, and I returned home. To say that it was great to come home is an understatement. What a joy to be reunited with our children and grandchildren. We had four grandchildren born while we were on our mission and two more were added through adoption. Getting to know them has been incredible. Beyond the reunion with family and friends, there is the joy in being home, not under the same pressures and toils. There is a peace and joy and contentment that is real. Likewise, I have a new understanding of how time (or the lack of it) will work in the next life. Three years is a long, long time and yet at the same time is nothing but the blink of an eye. When we returned home from our mission, it didn't take long to feel as if we had never been gone. Yet we were different in many ways because of our experiences. I think when we pass through the veil into the spirit world it will be much the same.

One of the great heartaches that my mother and father experienced in this life was the death of a child. Next to the graves of my Mom and Dad is a small grave that holds the earthly remains of my brother whom I never knew in mortality. He died as a four-day-old baby. What is the spirit world like for him? What is he doing now? I am sure that every parent who has lost a child has wondered those same things. The restored gospel gives us some valuable insight and profound comfort regarding this subject. President Joseph F. Smith declared: "The spirits of our children are immortal before they come to us, and their spirits, after bodily death, are like they were before they came. They are as they would have appeared if they had lived in the flesh, to grow to maturity, or to develop their physical bodies to the full stature of their spirits. If you see one of your children that has passed away it may appear to you in the form in which you would recognize it, the form of childhood; but if it came to you as a messenger bearing some important truth, it would come perhaps as the spirit of Bishop Edward Hunter's son (who died when a little child) came to him, in the stature of full-grown manhood, and revealed himself to his father, and said: 'I am your son.'

"Bishop Hunter did not understand it. He went to my father and said: 'Hyrum, what does that mean? I buried my son when he was only a little boy, but he has come to me as a full-grown man—a noble, glorious, young man, and declared himself my son. What does it mean?'

"Father (Hyrum Smith, the Patriarch) told him that the Spirit of Jesus Christ was full-grown before he was born into the world; and so our children were full-grown and possessed their full stature in the spirit, before they entered mortality, . . . and as they will also appear after the resurrection, when they shall have completed their mission."[6]

I find that so interesting and comforting. My brother that died as a baby is a full-grown, spiritually mature man now in the spirit world. If I were to see him today, that is how he would appear. Interestingly, most of the people who have had near-death experiences as children and glimpsed the spirit world recount that they saw themselves as adults. This was quite surprising to them. Dr. Raymond Moody, author of *Life after Life,* one of the classic books in this field (and who, I might add, is not of our faith), said, "a surprising number . . . say that they are adults . . . , although they can't say how they know this." To illustrate this, Moody quotes one woman who recalled: "In looking back at the experience, I realize that I was fully mature when I was in his presence. As I said, I was only seven, but I know I was an adult."[7] Fascinating!

I believe that my brother who died as a baby was indeed, as the Prophet Joseph Smith taught concerning little children who die before accountability, "too pure, too lovely to live on earth."[8] That doctrine comforts grieving mothers and fathers. I know it comforted my mother. In light of what the prophets have declared, I believe that my parents at their deaths were reunited with their son and are now laboring side by side with him in the great work of the Lord in the spirit world, sharing the gospel, teaching, blessing and strengthening others, and that he will continue that great service until the morning of the first resurrection. Then my mother and father will realize another one of the most comforting promises of the gospel, another kind of reunion. They will be able to raise my brother in the resurrection. When they come forth on the morning of the first resurrection, my mother will once again have a babe in arms to love and nurture and rear. President Joseph F. Smith stated: "Joseph Smith declared that the mother who laid down her little child, being deprived of the privilege, the joy, and the satisfaction of bringing it up to manhood or womanhood in this world, would, after the resurrection, have all the joy, satisfaction and pleasure, *and even more than it would have been possible to have had in mortality,* in seeing her child grow to the full measure of the stature of its spirit."[9]

I can only imagine the glorious reunion of my parents with their long-departed son. They had been separated for nearly sixty years. Reunion with loved ones is certainly one of the most significant and most joyful conditions of the spirit world. The Prophet Joseph himself looked forward to the joyful reunion with his loved ones on the other side of the veil of death. He said: "I have a father, brothers, children, and friends who have gone to the world of spirits. They are only absent for a moment. They are in the spirit, and we shall soon meet again. . . . When we depart [from this life], we shall hail our mothers, fathers, friends, and all whom we love, who have fallen asleep in Jesus. . . . It will be an eternity of felicity."[10] Brigham Young said: "We have more friends behind the vail than on this side, and they will hail us more joyfully than you were ever welcomed by your parents and friends in this world; and you will rejoice more when you meet them than you ever rejoiced to see a friend in this life."[11]

The doctrine of the spirit world being a place of joyous and loving reunion with family and friends is a glorious and comforting doctrine. President Joseph F. Smith said of this doctrine, "What is more desirable than that we should meet with our fathers and our mothers, with our brethren and our sisters, with our wives and our children, with our beloved associates and kindred in the spirit world, knowing each other, identifying each other . . . by the associations that familiarize each to the other in mortal life? What do you want better than that? What is there for any religion superior to that? I know of nothing."[12]

There is another kind of reunion with departed family members. It sometimes occurs even before we enter into the spirit world. The Prophet Joseph Smith taught that the more righteous a person is "the clearer are his views"[13] and the more he will understand God. Perhaps we can take that statement and say that the more righteous one becomes, the thinner the veil becomes. Under the influence of the Spirit, we may at times feel that the spirit world and those we love who are there are very close indeed. The Prophet Joseph Smith taught that our departed loved ones "are not far from us"[14] and that they continue to feel deeply about us. I am reminded of a story about Elder Bruce R. McConkie's father, Oscar W. McConkie Sr. When he was close to death, Brother McConkie called his family together at his bedside to express his love and give some departing counsel. He told them, "I am going to die. When I die, I shall not cease to love you. I shall not cease to pray for you. I shall not cease to labor in your behalf."[15]

It makes perfect sense to me that just as we continue to think about and love those who are separated from us by death, they continue to think about and love us. President Joseph F. Smith taught: "Sometimes the Lord expands our vision from this point of view and this side of the veil, that we feel and seem to realize that we can look beyond the thin veil which separates us from that other sphere. . . . [And we would understand that] those who have passed beyond, can see more clearly through the veil back here to us than it is possible for us to see them from our sphere of action. I believe we move and have our being in the presence of heavenly messengers and of heavenly beings. We are not separate from them. We begin to realize more and more fully, as we become acquainted with the principles of the Gospel, as they have been revealed anew in this dispensation, that we are closely related to our kindred, to our ancestors, to our friends and associates and co-laborers who have preceded us into the spirit world. We can not forget them; we do not cease to love them; we always hold them in our hearts, in memory, and thus are associated and united to them by ties that we cannot break, that we cannot dissolve or free ourselves from. . . . And therefore, I claim that we live in their presence, they see us, they are solicitous for our welfare, they love us now more than ever. For now they see the dangers that beset us; they can comprehend better than ever before, the weaknesses that are liable to mislead us into dark and forbidden paths. They see the temptations and evils that beset us in life and the proneness of mortal beings to yield to temptation and wrong doing; hence their solicitude for us and their love for us and their desire for our well being must be greater than that which we feel for ourselves."[16]

What a comforting thought it is to know that we are not alone in facing our challenges or dealing with our difficulties. President Ezra Taft Benson testified that "there are people over there who are pulling for us—people who have faith in us and who have great hopes for us, who are hoping and praying that we will measure up—our loved ones (parents, grandparents, brothers, sisters, and friends) who have passed on."[17] In Doctrine and Covenants 84:88, the Lord promised: "I will go before your face. I will be on your right hand and on your left, and my Spirit shall be in your hearts, *and mine angels round about you, to bear you up*" (emphasis added). You have probably read that passage many times, as I have. Perhaps you have wondered too: Who are those angels? Because of the restored gospel's teachings about the spirit world and eternal families, we know the answer. President Joseph F. Smith taught it clearly. He said: "When messengers are sent to minister to the inhabitants of this earth, they are not strangers, but from the ranks of our kindred [and] friends. . . . In like manner, our fathers and mothers, brothers, sisters and friends who have passed away from this earth, having been faithful, and worthy to enjoy these rights and privileges, may have a mission given to them to visit their relatives and friends upon the earth again, bringing from the divine Presence messages of love, of warning, or reproof and instruction, to those whom they had learned to love in the flesh."[18]

That makes perfect sense. If there is to be help from beyond the veil it will come from those who know and love us best and who desire to help us most. Do you realize what a blessing that can be to us as parents and grandparents, sons and daughters, brothers and sisters? Sometimes we know when the veil is being parted in our behalf, but most times we don't. Whether that help, that reunion, with loved ones is seen or unseen, it is real. Speaking specifically to parents who have children who have strayed from the path of righteousness, President James E. Faust not long before his own death gave this comforting assurance: "Perhaps in this life we are not given to fully understand how enduring the sealing cords of righteous parents are to their children. It may very well be that there are more helpful sources at work than we know. I believe there is a strong familial pull as the influence of beloved ancestors continues with us from the other side of the veil."[19]

I believe that I am a beneficiary of that promise. An experience in our family demonstrated to me that perhaps this kind of spiritual guidance and help from loved ones on the other side is what the Lord meant when he promised that he would "cause the heavens to shake for [our] good" (D&C 21:6).

Like many parents in the Church, we have had our share of challenges raising our children. Each child brings his or her own unique challenges. One of our children had veered quite a ways from the strait and narrow path and it seemed like nothing we did as parents could draw her back into the gospel fold. There was one thing, however, that could, and that was the influence of loving grandparents. Our daughter had a special relationship with my parents, particularly my father. She had so much love and respect for him. He seemed to be able to influence her in ways that we as her parents could not. Shortly after my father passed away, I left the hospital and went to his home. I stood all alone in his living room. My feelings were extremely tender as I gazed upon an anniversary photograph of my Mom and Dad taken on their sixtieth wedding anniversary. Mom had died only eighteen months before Dad. Hoping that they were both nearby, I spoke to them and told them how much I continued to need their influence in our family, particularly in the life of our teenage daughter. I hoped that, if they could, they would be able to part the veil in some way and touch her heart and help her find her way back. Several years and many miracles later, that daughter was married for time and all eternity in the Nauvoo Temple. While I don't know all that they were able to do from that side of the veil, there is no doubt in my mind that they were part of the "heavens [shaking] for [our] good." Though I did not see my Mom and Dad that day in the sealing room, the veil was very thin. I *knew* they and many others of our dear departed loved ones were with us, rejoicing with us, beaming with pride, and in some measure taking a little credit—credit I was glad to give them.

The Prophet Joseph Smith taught that those on the other side of the veil "cannot be made perfect" without us and "neither can we without our dead be made perfect." He often spoke of a "welding link" between the dead and the living (D&C 128:15, 18). It is clear from the Prophet's teachings that there is a salvational connection between the spirit world and this mortal existence. We know that this relates specifically to the work that goes on in our temples. But I think there is more to it than merely doing our genealogy and performing ordinances for those who did not have that privilege in this life. We do work for them, but they are doing work for us in ways that we may not always recognize. The work of the Lord, for our salvation and theirs, goes forth "nobly and boldly" on both sides of the veil. And all of this is for the intent to prepare us for the greatest and most glorious family reunion.

Chapter 6

LIFE REVIEW AND THE LAW OF RESTORATION

At death there is a partial judgment. To some degree, we will know our standing before the Lord when we enter the spirit world. I like to jokingly tell my students that if, when you die, there are a lot of people preaching *to* you, that is not a good sign. Of course, that is not doctrine—I am just joking. On a serious note, however, the gospel does indeed teach us some important things about judgment after death. John the Revelator declared that "the books [will be] opened. . . . and the dead [will be] judged out of those things which [are] written in the books, according to their works" (Revelation 20:12). In the Book of Mormon, the prophet Jacob declared that "when all men shall have passed from this first death unto life, . . . they must appear before the judgment-seat of the Holy One of Israel; and then cometh the judgment, and then must they be judged according to the holy judgment of God" (2 Nephi 9:15). Jacob also taught that, as part of that judgment in the next life, "we shall have a perfect knowledge of all our guilt, and our uncleanness, . . . and the righteous shall have a perfect knowledge of their enjoyment, and their righteousness, being clothed with purity, yea, even with the robe of righteousness" (2 Nephi 9:14). Alma also testified of that judgment including a "perfect remembrance" and a "bright recollection" of either our guilt or righteousness (Alma 5:18; 11:43). He further proclaimed that every aspect of our being will come weighed in the balance of judgment—that we will be judged by our thoughts, our words, and our deeds (see Mosiah 4:30; Alma 12:14). One of the most sobering scriptures concerning the judgment is found in the Doctrine and Covenants. The Lord tells us that "the rebellious shall be pierced with much sorrow; for their iniquities shall be spoken upon the housetops, and their secret acts shall be revealed" (D&C 1:3). How does that work?

Many of those who have had near-death experiences or encountered the spirit world in some manner speak of a sort of judgment that takes place there. They often speak of it as a "life review." The phrase, "my life passed before me," may be quite literal. I must admit that I have often thought that such a life review would be like watching a movie and that we will all get to watch each other's "life movies," the good, the bad, and the ugly. You might ask, Well, what if I have repented? Will we see the sins I've repented of also? I think the answer is no, but how it works I don't fully understand. If our sins are just blotted out on the movie, will there be lots of blank space on the video? I'm being a bit facetious here. I don't think our life review is a movie, necessarily, but it will be just as real; in fact, more real than a movie. Dr. George Ritchie described his post-mortal life review as directed by the "Being of Light" (whom he perceived was the Savior) this way: "When I say He knew everything about me, this was simply an observable fact. For into that room along with His radiant presence—simultaneously, though telling about it I have to describe them one by one—had also entered every single episode of my entire life. Everything that had ever happened to me was simply there, in full view, contemporary and current, all seemingly taking place at that moment."[1]

Another person who temporarily entered the spirit world and briefly experienced conditions there, described the life review in this manner: "It was like I knew everything that was stored in my brain. Everything I'd ever known from the beginning of my life I immediately knew about. And also what was kind of scary was that I knew everybody else in the room knew and I knew there was no hiding anything—the good times, the bad times, everything. . . . I had a total complete clear knowledge of everything that had ever happened in my life—even the little things that I had forgotten. . . . Everything was so clear."[2]

Do you see the parallel these experiences have to those scriptural phrases, "bright recollection," "perfect remembrance," and "awful view" (Mosiah 3:25)? Elder Orson Pratt said, "Things that may have been erased from your memory for years will be presented before you with all the vividness as if they had just taken place."[3] How can that be? President John Taylor explained it this way: "The spirit lives where the record of his deeds is kept—that does not die—man cannot kill it; there is no decay associated with it, and it still retains in all its vividness the remembrance of that which transpired before the separation by death of the body and the ever-living spirit. . . .

[At that judgment] it would be vain for a man to say then, I did not do so-and-so; the command would be, Unravel and read the record which he has made of himself, and let it testify in relation to these things, and *all could gaze upon it.* . . . That record will stare him in the face, he tells the story himself, and bears witness against himself. . . . When we get into the eternal world . . . [God's] eye can penetrate every one of us, and our own record of our lives here shall develop all."[4]

Do you see how, in this manner, as Alma said, "our words will condemn us, yea, all our works will condemn us; . . . and our thoughts will also condemn us; and in this awful state we shall not dare to look up to our God; and we would fain be glad if we could command the rocks and the mountains to fall upon us to hide us from his presence" (Alma 12:14). Let me share with you a personal experience, an embarrassing moment in my life, that gave me a small glimpse of what it means to have our sins "shouted from the housetops."

Many years ago when I first started my teaching career in the Church Educational System (back in the Stone Age before we had copy machines) I was preparing handouts for my next day's classes. I was hurrying because my wife, Wendy, was going to pick me up and we were going to attend a temple session. When I heard the honk of the car horn, I grabbed my suit coat and ran out the door of the seminary building. At the temple, we changed into our temple clothes. I kept on the white dress shirt I had worn that day. I put on my white pants and my white tie totally unaware that anything was wrong. To my horror, as I raised my arm during the endowment session I noticed a big, black ink spot on the sleeve of my white shirt. I had inadvertently put my arm in some ink that was used on the old mimeograph machine that made copies for us in those days. (In the "good old days," in order to make a copy of something, we had to type it on a stencil that was then attached to a cylinder and "run off.") In my haste, I had spilled some ink on the work counter and then put my arm in the spill. Can you imagine my embarrassment? I felt that everyone in the temple session was looking at me, observing the unsightly stain on my shirt. All were clothed in white, symbolic of personal purity, and yet there I stood in the midst of them with a hideous black blotch conspicuous in its contrast to the white robes surrounding me. I wanted to disappear. It was only an ink spot, but I felt unworthy. I have never forgotten how I felt at that time. I now understand a little better what it means to stand totally transparent—spiritually naked, if you will—before the Lord and others. We will be seen as we really are. There will be no hiding.

Emanuel Swedenborg spoke of this phenomenon and described what he had seen in the spirit world. In 1758, he wrote: "There were people who denied crimes and disgraceful things they had committed in the world. So lest people believe them innocent, all things were uncovered and reviewed out of their memory, in sequence, from their earliest age to the end. . . .

"There were some people who had taken others in by evil devices and who had stolen. Their wiles and thefts were recounted one after another—many of them things hardly anyone in the world had known other than the thieves themselves. . . .

"There were people who took bribes. . . . [Others had committed adultery and every kind of evil.] There was one person who thought nothing of disparaging others. I heard his disparaging remarks repeated in their sequence, his defamations as well, in the actual words—whom they were about, whom they were addressed to. All these elements were set forth and presented together in wholly life-like fashion; [even though] the details had been covered up by him while he had lived in the world. . . .

"In short, each evil spirit is shown clearly all his evil deeds, his crimes, thefts, deceits, and devices. These are brought out of his own memory and proven; there is no room left for denial, since all the attendant circumstances are visible at once. . . ."

Swedenborg then makes this final statement, the "moral of the story" or the meaning of what he had witnessed: "Let no one then believe that there is anything a person has thought within himself or done in secret that remains hidden after death. Let him rather believe that each and everything will then be visible as in broad daylight."[5]

It is fascinating to me to see how closely Swedenborg's description, along with the accounts of other non–Latter-day Saints who have had near-death experiences, coincide so closely with the scriptures and teachings of the latter-day prophets. It is fascinating but also sobering. Sobering, because these accounts so graphically confirm that we will not be able to hide from what we did and what we were. No wonder the Book of Mormon prophet Amulek taught in Alma chapter 34: "For behold, this life is the time for men to prepare to meet God; yea, behold the day of this life is the day for men to perform their labors. And now, as I said unto you before, as ye have had so many witnesses, therefore, I beseech of you that ye do not procrastinate the day of your repentance until the end" (Alma 34:32–33).

Clearly, one of the most important lessons we learn about life by studying death and the spirit world is the need for continual repentance. The English word *repentance* comes from the Hebrew and Greek words that mean literally "to turn"; to turn from sinfulness, to turn our backs on evil and temptation and turn toward God and strive each day to do better and to become better. As we do that, when our turn comes to have our life review on the other side of the veil, we will have a "bright recollection" of our goodness instead of an "awful view" of our wickedness. We will be seen as we really are, and through our faith and repentance, coupled with the sanctifying power of the Savior, our whole being is changed. Instead of being viewed by all as "natural" men and women, we will be seen as "new creatures in Christ" (see 2 Corinthians 5:17). In Doctrine and Covenants 58, the Lord declares: "Behold, he who has repented of his sins, the same is forgiven, and I, the Lord, remember them no more" (D&C 58:42). How thankful I am that because of the atonement of Jesus Christ my "life review" can be modified to feature the new me instead of the old one.

There is another aspect of that life review (the partial judgment that occurs in the spirit world) that has an important lesson for us here in mortality. Amulek not only taught that this life is the time to prepare to meet God and that we should not procrastinate the day of our repentance, but also explained why. He said: "Ye cannot say, when ye are brought to that awful crisis, that I will repent, that I will return to my God. Nay, ye cannot say this; for that same spirit which doth possess your bodies at the time that ye go out of this life, that same spirit will have power to possess your body in that eternal world"

(Alma 34:34). What does that mean? We know from the re-stored gospel that we take with us into the spirit world the same attitudes, dispositions, and desires we have here. What we love here we will love there. If we are drawn to evil here, we will be drawn to it there. If we love righteousness and the things of God here, so will we there. President Heber C. Kimball stated: "If men and women do not qualify themselves and become sanctified and purified in this life, they will go into the world of the spirits where they will have a greater contest with the devils than [they] had with them here."[6]

Repentance in this life prepares us for the next life. Repentance changes more than just behavior. It changes our very being, what we are at the very core: our desires, our at-titudes, our love and devotion. Procrastinating repentance here makes spiritual progression there far more difficult. Elder Melvin J. Ballard of the Quorum of the Twelve, in a classic address entitled "The Three Degrees of Glory," given in 1922, said: "This life is the time in which men are to repent. Do not let any of us imagine that we can go down to the grave not having overcome the corruptions of the flesh and then lose in the grave all our sins and evil tendencies. They will be with us. They will be with the spirit when separated from the body.

"It is my judgment that any man or woman can do more to conform to the laws of God in one year in this life than they could do in ten years when they are dead. . . . It is much easier to overcome sin and serve the Lord when both the flesh and spirit are combined as one. . . . We will find when we are dead every desire, every feeling will be greatly intensified. . . . [Therefore], every man and woman who is putting off until the next life the task of correcting and overcoming the weaknesses of the flesh are sentencing themselves to years of bondage, for no man or woman will come forth in the resurrection until they have completed their work, until they have [repented] and overcome [evil], until they have done as much as they can do. . . . Those who are [repenting and obeying] in this life are shortening [that period of time], for every one of us will have [a period of time] in that spirit state to complete and finish our salvation."[7]

No wonder we are counseled not to procrastinate our repentance—procrastinating repentance is prolonging suffering and delaying the joy, peace, blessings, and glory that await us in the world to come. Just as disobedience, sin, and an unwillingness to repent in this life will slow spiritual progress in the next world, faithfulness, repentance, and obedience here will expedite and expand our progress there.

There is a principle taught in the scriptures in several different contexts that I call the "Law of Reciprocity." We have a saying in our modern vernacular for this law: "What goes around comes around." A great example of that is found in the Sermon on the Mount when the Savior said: "Judge not unrighteously, for with what judgment ye judge, ye shall be judged: and with what measure ye mete, it shall be measured to you again" (JST, Matthew 7:2). The Apostle Paul stated that "whatsoever a man soweth, that shall he also reap" (Galatians 6:7). We today often refer to this idea as the "law of the harvest." To the Galatians, Paul wrote: "Be not deceived; God is not mocked: . . . Let us not be weary in well doing: for in due season we shall reap" (Galatians 6:7, 9). In the Book of Mormon, the prophet Alma referred to it as "restoration." In Alma 41, Alma taught his son Corianton regarding this principle: "And it is requisite with the justice of God that men should be judged according to their works; and if their works were good in this life, and the desires of their hearts were good, that they should also, at the last day, be restored unto that which is good.

"And if their works are evil they shall be restored unto them for evil. . . .

"The one raised to happiness according to his desires of happiness, or good according to his desires of good; and the other to evil according to his desires of evil; for as he has desired to do evil all the day long even so shall he have his reward of evil when the night cometh" (Alma 41:3–5).

We see how this works in life to a limited degree. But in the spirit world this facet of the law of restoration is an absolutely perfect and just return for our actions in life. We get what we gave. We reap what we sowed. We experience all the effects of our own choices. Those who have glimpsed beyond the veil of death and have experienced the partial judgment associated with a life review provide us with some fascinating observations. Let me share with you a few of those accounts. One person said, "It was not my life [that] passed before me [and it was certainly not merely] a three-dimensional caricature of the events in my life. What occurred was every emotion I have ever felt in life, I felt. And my eyes were showing me the basis of how that emotion affected my life."[8] One woman said that as part of her life review she not only saw herself in her second grade class, but she also could smell the classroom and hear the sounds. It was perfect sensory recall. But one thing really stood out. In that view of her life, she saw her teacher whom she greatly disliked accidentally fall off a chair while pinning something to the bulletin board and writhe in pain on the floor. What she remembered most was the terrible guilt she felt for having laughed when her teacher fell. Her judgment of herself during her life review involved seeing, smelling, hearing, but most of all *feeling* the feelings of hating another and of taking joy in another's pain and misfortune.[9] Another person who had gone into the spirit world described it this way: "Mine was not a review, it was a reliving. For me, it was a total reliving of every thought I had ever thought, every word I had ever spoken, and every deed I had ever done; *plus* the effect of each thought, word, and deed on everyone and anyone who had ever come within my environment or sphere of influence whether I knew them or not."[10]

"When I would see something," recounted one man concerning his life review, "when I would experience a past event, it was like I was seeing it through eyes with . . . omnipotent knowledge, guiding me, and helping me to see. That's the part that has stuck with me, because it showed me not only what I had done but even how what I had done had affected other people."[11] These glimpses beyond the veil, coupled with scriptures and the teachings of the prophets, provide us with a sobering insight into the literal and profound nature of the law of restoration.

Chapter 7

THINGS THAT MATTER MOST

One of the most important lessons learned by those people who have glimpsed beyond the veil of death is what is most important and lasting in life. It often brings a radical re-ordering of their priorities in mortality. These glimpses into the spirit world remind us that one of the greatest blessings of the restored gospel of Jesus Christ is that we know which things matter most; what our eternal priorities *should* be.

In the Sermon on the Mount, the Savior taught, "Lay not up for yourselves treasures upon earth, where moth and rust doth corrupt, and where thieves break through and steal: but lay up for yourselves treasures in heaven, . . . for where your treasure is, there will your heart be also" (Matthew 6:19–21). At another time, he taught, "For what is a man profited, if he shall gain the whole world, and lose his own soul? or what shall a man give in exchange for his soul?" (Matthew 16:26). The contrast between earthly treasures and eternal riches was dramatically seen in Emanuel Swedenborg's spirit world visions.

He described those spirits who had spent their entire lives seeking after and serving the materialistic "gods of this world," instead of the God of the Universe, as being the most poor and spiritually bankrupt in the world to come. Those people on earth who adorned themselves with costly apparel and jewels but ignored God and oppressed the poor were actually clothed in rags. In contrast, those who may not have had much in mortality but who diligently sought after righteousness were clothed with robes of glory. They were the ones who were truly rich.[1] Isn't that an interesting idea? It certainly correlates with what the scriptures, both ancient and modern, teach us about seeking first the kingdom of God.

Perhaps Nephi's description of those who "fight against Zion" could also be applied to those in mortality who spend their time, effort, energy, and resources in pursuit of what I like to call "the mirage of materialism." When they find themselves on the other side, "it shall be unto them, even as unto a hungry man which dreameth, and behold he eateth but he awaketh and his soul is empty; or like unto a thirsty man which dreameth, and behold he drinketh but he awaketh and behold he is faint, and his soul [still] hath appetite" (2 Nephi 27:3). And as Isaiah counseled, "Do not spend money for that which is of no worth, nor your labor for that which cannot satisfy" (2 Nephi 9:51; see also Isaiah 55:2). Instead, as the Lord declared in our day: "Seek not for riches but for wisdom, and behold, the mysteries of God shall be unfolded unto you, and then shall you be made rich. Behold, he that hath eternal life is rich" (D&C 6:7).

It seems as if a brush with death or another major trauma in life forces us to reevaluate our priorities and take a serious inventory of ourselves. We saw that on 9/11. We experience it in our own lives when we face serious illness or lose a loved one. Likewise, it seems that anyone who is privileged to glimpse the spirit world comes away from the experience profoundly transformed and their recognition of what matters most in life profoundly affected. People who have had near-death experiences with the spirit world often have a difficult time readjusting to life back in mortality.

In some ways, it reflects our challenge "to be in the world, but not of the world."[2] One woman recalled this difficulty. She said: "I can recall in my attempt to hold onto the feeling [of] peace [I had experienced in the spirit world]. I began to bump into earthly things that you know, of course, aren't going to escape from you—they're there. My first frustrating experience was with television. I couldn't watch television. There would be a commercial, a cosmetic commercial, I couldn't—. I'd have to turn it off because it was something false, it was unnecessary, it was fake. It just didn't belong, [it was] insignificant. Any type of violence . . . even an old Western movie, I'd have to turn it off because to me it was total ignorance. There was just no reason on earth to show people killing people."[3]

It is interesting to note that most of the people who encountered the spirit world and who had experienced the glory of the next estate came back from that experience with a new sense of purpose and priorities in life. Many changed professions, often into service-related fields, because they understood that relationships were more important and eternal than making a good living, and that people are always more important than things. One person said: "I gained a lot of understanding [from my experience]. I saw that we're moving so fast in our society, we're not taking time to look at what God has given us. We're not getting to know people, which is the essence of what it's all about. We're not here to be making millions of dollars and getting to the top of the corporate ladder. That's not what God wants us to do. We're here for people."[4]

Another person who had a near-death experience described the changes that took place in him after his "visit" to the spirit world: "My joy comes from another's smile. I also notice that I reach out and touch people more. . . . I have more insight into other people [now]. . . . It's very difficult for me to lose my temper anymore. I can see the pain in other people's eyes. That's why they hurt other people because they really don't understand. . . . The most important thing that we have are our relationships with other people. . . . It all comes down to caring and compassion and love for your fellowman. . . . *Love is the answer. It's the answer to everything.*"[5]

A common thread through all of the many accounts of people's glimpses into the spirit world is that of love, an increased love for God and the things of the Spirit and an increased love for one's fellowman. Isn't that really what Jesus taught when he was asked, "What is the greatest commandment?" He said that upon two things "hang all the law and the prophets" (Matthew 22:40), which was His way of saying to a Jewish audience, "everything hinges on these two things": first and foremost, loving God, and *then* loving others—our family, friends, neighbors, strangers, everyone—including our enemies (see Matthew 22:36–39). The Apostle Paul in the New Testament and the prophet Mormon in the Book of Mormon both testified of the preeminence of divine love in heaven and on earth. Paul wrote to the Corinthian Saints: "Though

I speak with the tongues of men and of angels, and have not charity, I am become as sounding brass, or a tinkling cymbal. And though I have the gift of prophecy, and understand all mysteries, and all knowledge; and though I have all faith, so that I could remove mountains, and have not charity, I am nothing. And though I bestow all my goods to feed the poor, and though I give my body to be burned, and have not charity, it profiteth me nothing" (1 Corinthians 13:1–3).

Mormon likewise testified: "Wherefore, my beloved brethren, if ye have not charity, ye are nothing, for charity never faileth. Wherefore, cleave unto charity, *which is the greatest of all,* for all things must fail—but charity is the pure love of Christ, and it endureth forever; and whoso is found possessed of it at the last day, it shall be well with him" (Moroni 7:46–47; emphasis added).

The two most commonly cited words to describe the spirit world by both Latter-day Saints and those not of our faith are *light* and *love*—and they always go hand in hand. The light and glory that fills our souls and radiates in God's realm is also God's perfect love. Here are just a few of the accounts of people who experienced that perfect light and love in their encounters with the spirit world:

"Love is the major impression I still retain. In heaven there is light, peace, music, beauty and joyful activity, but above all there is love and within this love I felt more truly alive than I have ever done before."[6]

"There was the warmest, most wonderful love. Love all around me. . . . I felt light-good-happy-joy-at ease. Forever—eternal love. Time meant nothing. Just being. Love. Pure love. Love."[7]

This is an interesting glimpse of the righteous spirits on the other side of the veil: "Seeing these beings and feeling the joy, peace and happiness which swelled up from them made me feel that here was the place of all places, the top realm of all realms. These beings who inhabited it were full of love."[8]

And lastly, "I also felt and saw of course that everyone was in a state of absolute compassion to everything else. . . . It seemed, too, that love was the major axiom that everyone automatically followed. . . . There was nothing but love. . . . [It was] the real thing, just to feel this sense of total love in every direction."[9]

As I read these descriptions of the light and love that prevail on the other side, I immediately thought of Lehi's and Nephi's descriptions of the fruit of the tree of life, which is the love of God. Lehi said that "it filled my soul with exceedingly great joy" (1 Nephi 8:12). Nephi declared that the love of God "is the most desirable above all things" (1 Nephi 11:22). It is this perfect and exquisite love that caused Brigham Young to say that he had to exercise far greater faith to continue to live in mortality after he had tasted of what he called "the glory of the next apartment."[10] Likewise, it is this incredible light and love that led to Jedediah M. Grant saying that the greatest dread he had ever had was to return to his body after being in the spirit world, even for a short time.[11] Numerous others, some not even of our faith, have had similar experiences. Speaking of a Being of Light, one person said: "What the light communicates to you is a feeling of true, pure love. You experience this for the first time ever. You can't compare it to the love of your wife, or the love of your children. . . . Even if all [the things you love] were combined you cannot compare it to the feeling of love you get from this light."[12]

Many spoke of how the love they felt in the spirit world has now powerfully affected them in life. They try to love others more and try to live so as to be able to once again be embraced in that perfect love—*forever.* As one man who is not of our faith observed: "Going into that Light is a beautiful feeling in that you feel love and forgiveness. To not be able to stay in that realm of heavenly love would be hell. To experience it, to know it's there, and not be able to partake of it: That's hell."[13] Interestingly, Elder Orson Pratt taught that hell is the total absence of God's perfect love. [14] As I ponder his words I wonder if *hell* or what we often refer to as "outer darkness" is not only the absence of *light,* but also the total and absolute void of Light's eternal companion, Love.[15] All who have experienced this infinite light and love—these "better worlds and greater light"— know that they are indeed the great motivators. Elder Melvin J. Ballard, who partook of the pure love of Christ in a dream wherein he was embraced and kissed by the Savior, recounted: "The feeling that came into my heart then was: Oh! if I could live worthy, though it would require four-score years, so that in the end when I have finished I could go into His presence and receive the feeling that I then had in His presence, I would give everything that I am and ever hope to be!"[16]

Although we may not have that kind of manifestation and we may not in this life obtain a literal vision of the spirit world, we can still feel the pull of God's light and love. Knowledge of the gospel of Jesus Christ gives us valuable insight into the Plan of Salvation. Partaking of Christ's love through his Atonement provides the greatest motivation. The more we feel of his love in our lives the more we long to live in such a way as to experience that perfect love in its fulness forever. In a similar manner, the more we taste of that fruit that is "most desirable above all things," the more love we will share with those around us—our families, our friends, our fellowmen.

Chapter 8

LIVING TO DIE

The ancient Egyptians believed strongly in an afterlife
and much of their mortal existence was in preparation
for that other world. But their preparation was much different
from what the gospel teaches. Their preparation consisted in
building tombs to house their mortal remains and monuments
so their names would never be forgotten. Every imaginable
earthly possession was collected to be put in the tomb so that
they could be used by the deceased in the next life, including
gold, jewels, furniture, food, drink, and even ships or other
modes of transportation that would take the person to the
other world. I have been in many of those tombs in Egypt and
have seen all of the trappings that would be associated with
their preparations for death. They are amazing and even a little
overwhelming. Yet it seems like a waste in many ways, because
we know that you can't take material things with you.

While it may be easy to scoff at the ancient Egyptians and
think how silly it was for them to spend their entire lifetime

building and preparing their funeral tombs, there is, nonetheless, a valuable lesson we can learn from them. That lesson is preparation for death and the next life. While we recognize that true preparation is much different from merely building monuments, we can see that preparing to pass into the next world requires more than passing or periodic interest or casual effort.

For ancient Egyptian royalty, preparing for death was a lifetime pursuit, albeit in ways that would not matter much to us. The kind of preparation needed to faithfully enter into the next estate should likewise receive our continual effort. In reality, every moment of our earthly life is a preparation, in one way or another, for death. Just as death opens the door to life, life determines what death will be like. Thus, we are indeed — living to die.

President Harold B. Lee once said: "What we are *hereafter* depends on what we're *after here.*"[1] I like that play on words. Let me say it in a little different way: "What we *know* about the hereafter can influence what we *do* and *become* here after." Or another way of saying it: "Our knowledge of what it will be like *then* and *there* helps us to know what we should be like *here* and *now.*" The restored gospel of Jesus Christ doesn't just teach us about and prepare us for eternity; that preparation also blesses and enriches our lives right now. That is certainly true in regard to the doctrine of death and the spirit world.

Gospel insights about *dying* teach us a great deal about *living.* The scriptures teach that "if ye are prepared ye shall not fear" (D&C 38:30). Not only biologically, but spiritually, we begin preparation for death the moment we are born. How we live is how we prepare. Epictetus, the first-century

Greek philosopher, taught: "Keep death . . . daily before thine eyes. . . . then wilt thou never think a mean thought, nor covet anything beyond measure."[2] I like that phrase "keep death . . . daily before thine eyes." It may sound morbid to say "Think about death all the time." But we can "keep death daily before [our] eyes" by keeping our eyes focused on eternity and those things that matter most. In our day, the Lord declared: "Let the solemnities of eternity rest upon your minds" (D&C 43:34). That is the way whereby we are not only better prepared to die, but also better equipped to really live.

While many in the mortal world do not like to think about death and dying, the restored gospel of Jesus Christ, by its teachings and ordinances, keeps it before our eyes so that we will not forget that this life is not really our home and that each day we must be preparing to return to our *real* home, our eternal home. Think of the many ways in the Church and through gospel living whereby we are continually reminded of our mortality and of the need to prepare for and be worthy of what President Hinckley called "better worlds and greater light." When we are *living* as we should we are preparing for *dying,* which makes *life* all the more abundant and joyous.

There are two places in particular where we feel the closeness of the spirit world and where we are reminded most profoundly of the need to prepare for death. They are at funerals and in the temple.

My wife, Wendy, loves funerals. I tease her that she ought to read the obituaries in the newspaper and then just randomly select a funeral to attend. Like "an apple a day," she could attend a funeral a day. She probably would do that and really enjoy it. She finds funerals enjoyable because they often are celebrations of lives well lived and always are reminders of things that matter most. She loves the feeling of closeness to the Spirit that attends funerals.

How are we benefited by attending funerals? What role can they play in our own preparation for death? Perhaps the answer can be found in the fact that at funerals our hearts are more tender and our minds are more focused on our mortality. "One of the most solemn and sacred meetings of the Church is the funeral for a departed member," President Boyd K. Packer taught. "I know of no meeting where the congregation is in a better state of readiness to receive revelation and inspiration."[3] I add my own testimony to that. I have felt the Spirit powerfully testifying of the truths of the gospel at funerals. For me, there is probably more spiritual introspection at a funeral service than any other time (except maybe during the administration of the sacrament). Speaking at a funeral, President Howard W. Hunter said: "In the quiet of this chapel today, our souls have been on their knees. We have contemplated the uncertainties of life and the certainty of death. Each of us in his turn will follow the same course—only the point of time is the difference. Will we be ready? Will the things we intend to accomplish be completed? Will we make right the little wrongs and replace the harsh words with kindness before our call comes? Will we accept the fullness of the gospel of Jesus Christ by following his teachings, keeping his commandments, being of service to our fellowman, ready to enter the tomb, partake of the glorious resurrection, and stand at the judgment as worthy servants?"[4]

Those are important questions that we all need to frequently consider. Funerals aid us in much-needed soul searching. Not long ago, I attended the funeral service of a dear friend and colleague. It was deeply moving and the Spirit was there in rich abundance. Most touching were the tributes paid by his children. There was no mention of his positions of prominence or scholarly publications. Little was said of his career contributions. Instead the focus was totally on his love for others, his thoughtfulness and kindness, his roles as husband, father, and grandfather, and most of all, his faith and devotion to the Lord Jesus Christ. As I left that funeral, I wondered what my family and friends would say about me. What mark am I leaving in this world in the hearts and lives of those around me? Are my priorities right? Am I putting first things first or am I distracted and diverted, pursuing things that when the moment of death comes will not seem very important at all? As I took spiritual inventory of my life, I realized that every day, every moment I am writing my own eulogy. My words, my actions, my thoughts, my love are being written in my heart and soul and are likewise being recorded in the hearts of my family and fellowmen. If I don't like how that eulogy is being written, then I need to change it, and I can do that through repentance and striving to do better and be better. That is one of the great blessings of the gospel. Daily preparing for *dying,* as strange as that may sound, powerfully affects our daily *living.* As Shakespeare wrote: "Be absolute for death; either death or life / Shall thereby be the sweeter."[5]

A second way whereby we can have "death daily before [our] eyes" is through participation in the ordinances of the temple. I have heard it said that temples are where heaven and earth meet—the crossroads between mortality and eternity. Everything we do in the temple is focused on preparing for the next life and enriching our lives here and now. Our minds are continually centered on the relationship between the two. From the time we are assigned the name of a deceased person for whom we act as proxy to when we pass through the veil, which is a profound symbol, we are continually reminded in the temple about death as a gateway to immortality and eternal life. Even as we are focused on that next life and those in the spirit world, we are also reminded by instruction and covenant of the importance of this life and how living in harmony with those eternal principles will bless our own lives and families here and now. What a blessing it is to have temples and temple ordinances to keep our minds centered on the things of eternity. President Gordon B. Hinckley taught: "The Lord has made it possible for us in these holy houses to receive our own [ordinances]. Then we have the opportunity and responsibility of extending these same blessings to those who have passed on without the privilege. But in the process there comes into our own lives a refinement of character, together with increased spirituality. It is interesting to reflect on the fact that although many on the other side may not receive the ordinances done for them here, those who perform these ordinances will be blessed in the very process of doing so."[6]

On another occasion, President Hinckley promised that if we would worthily attend the temple on a regular basis "we will be a better people, we will be better fathers and husbands, we will be better wives and mothers." He then added this: "I know your lives are busy. I know that you have much to do. But I make you a promise that if you will go to the House of the Lord, you will be blessed; *life will be better for you.*"[7]

President Hinckley's promise about temples reminds me

of a principle that I often teach my students. I like to call it the principle of indirection. You find it in the scriptures a great deal; it's just not called that. The principle works this way: you focus on one thing, and another thing results. Like a boomerang—you throw it one direction and it comes back from the other. The most famous example in the scriptures of this is Matthew 10:39—"He that findeth his life shall lose it: and he that loseth his life for my sake shall find it." This is a seeming contradiction. Those who spend their lives focused solely on this life—living for now, giving little thought about what lies beyond—will come to realize that they have "lost the substance while seeking after the shadow." In a spiritual way, focusing only on *today* diminishes our *tomorrow.* In contrast, if we prepare for eternity each day of our lives, we will not only obtain eternal life, "better worlds and greater light," but our here and now will also be abundantly enhanced.

Several years ago, as my parents were getting older and slowing down considerably, I invited them to come and visit us in Utah. Mother's health wasn't good and she responded, "I don't know if we can come next week, because I don't know what next week will bring. We are just living day by day." I thought a great deal about that phrase, "We are just living day by day." Each of us, whether we are nine or ninety, is, in reality, living day by day. I may have plans and goals for weeks and months and years to come but nonetheless my life is in the Lord's hands. For me, the phrase "living day by day" doesn't mean that I don't have a long-range view. In fact, it is just the opposite. "Living day by day" means doing everything each day with an eternal perspective—recognizing that *today* might be "*the* day" when I am called home.

One of the most commonly expressed sentiments of those who have glimpsed beyond the veil during a near-death experience is that each of us has a purpose for our lives here on earth. Many of these people were told that they could not stay in the spirit world because they had not yet completed their mission in mortality. As Latter-day Saints we know that there is indeed a purpose to our existence. We believe strongly that before we ever came here we were foreordained for specific purposes, assignments, and opportunities to grow personally and to serve and strengthen others. While we may not always know the specific nature or duration of every purpose for which we were sent to this earth, we *will* fulfill those foreordained missions *if* we live worthily. The knowledge that we will report our stewardship and assess how we did in fulfilling our purposes in life should guide our direction and decisions in life and inspire us to do our best each day we live. President Spencer W. Kimball stated: "God has endowed us with talents and time, with latent abilities and with opportunities to use and develop them in his service. He therefore expects much of us, his privileged children."[8] Elsewhere he said, "The great calamity, as I see it, is when you and I with so much potential grow very little. That is the calamity—when I could be so much and I am so little; when I am satisfied with mediocrity."[9] He also taught: "[Therefore], let us get our instruments tightly strung and our melodies sweetly sung. Let us not die with our music still in us. Let us rather use this precious mortal probation to move confidently and gloriously upward toward eternal life which God our Father gives to those who keep his commandments."[10]

In the first chapter, I shared with you a statement from the Prophet Joseph Smith wherein he counseled us to study death, the spirit world, the Resurrection, and other principles of the Plan of Salvation "both day and night." As I now conclude, I return to that counsel. Studying implies not just reading and learning, but also pondering and living. If we ponder and live "both day and night" the truths of the gospel regarding our eternal existence, particularly where we want to spend the rest of our eternal lives, we will not only be better prepared for *dying,* but better prepared and equipped for real *living.* Elder Orson Pratt, like President Brigham Young and others of the early Brethren, spoke often about death and the conditions we will find in the spirit world. He explained to the Saints why he felt so strongly about that doctrine: "And do not forget to look forward to those joys ahead, if we do [forget], we will become careless, dormant, and sluggish, and we will think we do not see much ahead to be anticipated, but if we keep our minds upon the prize that lays ahead—upon the vast fields of knowledge to be poured out upon the righteous, and the glories that are to be revealed, and the heavenly things in the future state, we shall be continually upon the alert; . . . Let these things sink down in our minds continually, and they will make us joyful, and careful to do unto our neighbors as we would they should do unto us. Lest we should come short of some of these things is the reason I have touched upon the future state of man the two Sabbaths past, to stir up the pure minds of the Saints that we may prepare for the things that are not far ahead, and let all the actions of our lives have a bearing in relation to the future."[11]

May we prepare ourselves for that inevitable day. May we, as the great American poet William Cullen Bryant penned in his classic poem "Thanatopsis":

So live, that when thy summons comes to join
The innumerable caravan, which moves
To that mysterious realm, where each shall take
His chamber in the silent halls of death,
Thou go not, like the quarry-slave at night,
Scourged to his dungeon, but, sustained and soothed
By an unfaltering trust, approach thy grave,
Like one who wraps the drapery of his couch
About him, and lies down to pleasant dreams.[12]

I bear testimony of "better worlds and greater light" that await us when we depart from this life. I bear testimony of the truthfulness of the restored gospel—the gospel that teaches us so much about the real meaning of dying and living. Though sadness at separation always accompanies death, I am grateful that the gospel teaches us that someday "God shall wipe away all tears from [our] eyes" (Revelation 7:17). In place of loss and loneliness, there will indeed come "better worlds and greater light" because of the Atonement of Jesus Christ, the Son of God. I know He lives. I know that because He lives—"there is no death, but only change." How grateful I am for the peace the gospel brings. President Gordon B. Hinckley poetically, yet profoundly, declared:

O God, touch Thou my aching heart,
And calm my troubled, haunting fears.
Let hope and faith, transcendent, pure,
Give strength and peace beyond my tears.
There is no death, but only change
With recompense for victory won;

The gift of Him who loved all men,
The Son of God, the Holy One.[13]

I add my testimony to his words and those of the Apostle Paul: "O death, where is thy sting? O grave, where is thy victory? . . . Thanks be to God, which giveth us the victory through our Lord Jesus Christ" (1 Corinthians 15:55, 57).

NOTES

PREFACE

1. Hunter, "The Gospel—A Global Faith," 19.
2. First Presidency, "Statement of the First Presidency," February 15, 1978, in Palmer, *Expanding Church*, [v].
3. Young, *Discourses of Brigham Young*, 3.
4. Emerson, *Representative Men*, 60.

CHAPTER 1: DYING TO LIVE

1. Larson and Larson, *Diary of Charles Lowell Walker*, 1:465–66.
2. Joseph Smith, *History of the Church*, 6:50.
3. Hinckley, "The Empty Tomb Bore Testimony," 66.
4. *Teachings of Spencer W. Kimball*, 39.
5. Morse with Perry, *Transformed by the Light*, 64.
6. Packer, address at funeral of Gary Willis, June 4, 1971, in *Mine Errand from the Lord*, 34.
7. Brigham Young, in *Journal of Discourses*, 17:142.

CHAPTER 2: THE IMMORTAL SPIRIT

1. First Presidency, "The Origin of Man," 29.

2. Rogo, *Return from Silence,* 162.

3. Swedenborg, *Heaven and Hell,* 70–71.

4. See Packer, *Teach Ye Diligently,* 230–37.

5. Brigham Young, in *Journal of Discourses,* 9:287.

6. Orson Pratt, in *Journal of Discourses,* 15:242–43.

7. Young, in *Journal of Discourses,* 14:231.

8. Dr. Elisabeth Kübler-Ross, quoted in Zaleski, *Otherworld Journeys,* 116–17.

9. Unnamed author, quoted in Moody, *Life after Life,* 53.

10. See Ring and Cooper, *Mindsight.*

11. Parley P. Pratt, in *Journal of Discourses,* 1:8.

12. Young, in *Journal of Discourses,* 13:77.

13. Ibid., 14:231.

14. Maxwell, "Patience," 220.

15. *Teachings of the Prophet Joseph Smith,* 355.

16. Parley P. Pratt, in *Journal of Discourses,* 3:100–101.

17. Swedenborg, *Heaven and Hell,* 172–73.

18. Young, in *Journal of Discourses,* 8:10.

19. Orson Pratt, in *Journal of Discourses,* 2:247.

20. Ibid., 2:246.

21. Ibid., 2:239.

22. *Teachings of the Prophet Joseph Smith,* 324.

23. Smith, *History of the Church,* 6:52; emphasis added.

Chapter 3: The Spirit World

1. Brigham Young, in *Journal of Discourses,* 3:369.

2. Pratt, *Key to the Science of Theology,* 126–27.

3. Daisy Dryden, quoted in Rogo, *Return from Silence,* 47–48.

4. Rawlings, *Beyond Death's Door,* 38.

5. Peale, "There Is No Death," 7–9.

6. Joseph F. Smith, in Conference Report, April 1916, 2–3.

7. Young, in *Journal of Discourses,* 7:239.

8. Heber C. Kimball, in *Journal of Discourses,* 4:135–36.

9. Hale, "Everyone Had Something to Do," in Nelson, *Beyond the Veil*, 1:48–51.

10. Morse with Perry, *Transformed by the Light*, 82.

11. Mr. Dippong, quoted in Ring, *Heading toward Omega*, 64.

12. Unnamed author, quoted in Ring, "Amazing Grace," 29.

13. J.W. Skilton, quoted in Rogo, *Return from Silence*, 62.

14. Young, *Discourses of Brigham Young*, 242.

15. Swedenborg, *Heaven and Hell*, 137.

16. Swedenborg, *Heaven and Hell*, 141–42.

17. *Discourses of Brigham Young*, 380.

18. Swedenborg, *Heaven and Hell*, 170.

19. Ritchie with Sherrill, *Return from Tomorrow*, 54.

20. Moody, *Life after Life*, 64.

21. Sabom, *Recollections of Death*, 49.

22. *Teachings of Ezra Taft Benson*, 35–36.

23. Brigham Young Collection, February 17, 1847.

24. Heber C. Kimball, in *Journal of Discourses*, 4:135–36.

25. Hale, "Everyone Had Something to Do," in Nelson, *Beyond the Veil*, 1:48–49.

26. Swedenborg, *Heaven and Hell*, 160.

27. Unnamed author, quoted in Rogo, *Return from Silence*, 232.

28. Unnamed author, quoted in Ring, *Heading toward Omega*, 82.

CHAPTER 4: MINISTERS OF THE GOSPEL

1. *Discourses of Wilford Woodruff*, 288–89.

2. Ibid., 77.

3. Joseph F. Smith, *Gospel Doctrine*, 461; emphasis added.

4. Maxwell, *Notwithstanding My Weakness*, 55.

5. Snow, "Discourse by President Lorenzo Snow," quoted in Mouritsen, "The Spirit World, Our Next Home," 48.

6. Brigham Young, in *Journal of Discourses*, 3:94.

7. Parley P. Pratt, in *Journal of Discourses*, 1:9.

8. Cannon, *Gospel Truth*, 60.

9. Hale, "Everyone Had Something to Do," in Nelson, *Beyond the Veil,* 1:49.

10. *Teachings of the Prophet Joseph Smith,* 208.

CHAPTER 5: WELCOME HOME

1. Brigham Young, in *Journal of Discourses,* 4:268.

2. IANDS Conference, Experiencers Panel Discussion Transcript, 1990, 6–7.

3. Janis, quoted in Ring, *Heading toward Omega,* 60.

4. Mr. Dippong, quoted in Ring, *Heading toward Omega,* 64; emphasis added.

5. Unnamed author, quoted in Grey, *Return from Death,* 46–47.

6. Joseph F. Smith, *Gospel Doctrine,* 455.

7. Moody, *Light Beyond,* 74, 76.

8. Joseph Smith, *Joseph Smith,* 176.

9. Joseph F. Smith, *Gospel Doctrine,* 453; emphasis added.

10. Joseph Smith, *History of the Church,* 6:316.

11. Young, in *Journal of Discourses,* 6:349.

12. Joseph F. Smith, quoted in Millet and McConkie, *Life Beyond,* 26–27.

13. Joseph Smith, *History of the Church,* 2:8.

14. *Teachings of the Prophet Joseph Smith,* 326.

15. Cited in Millet, *When a Child Wanders,* 133.

16. Joseph F. Smith, in Conference Report, April 1916, 2–3.

17. *Teachings of Ezra Taft Benson,* 31.

18. Joseph F. Smith, *Gospel Doctrine,* 435–36.

19. Faust, "Dear Are the Sheep That Have Wandered," 62.

CHAPTER 6: LIFE REVIEW AND THE LAW OF RESTORATION

1. Ritchie with Sherrill, *Return from Tomorrow,* 49–50.

2. Hank, quoted in Ring, *Heading toward Omega,* 68–69.

3. Orson Pratt, in *Journal of Discourses,* 2:239.

4. John Taylor, in *Journal of Discourses,* 11:78–79; emphasis added.

5. Swedenborg, *Heaven and Hell,* 361–64.

6. Heber C. Kimball, in *Journal of Discourses,* 3:230.

7. Melvin J. Ballard, quoted in Crowther, *Life Everlasting,* 21–22.

8. Darryl, quoted in Ring, *Heading toward Omega,* 71.

9. See Harris and Bascom, *Full Circle,* 25.

10. Unnamed author, quoted in Atwater, *Coming Back to Life,* 36.

11. Unnamed author, quoted in Moody, *Reflections on Life after Life,* 35.

CHAPTER 7: THINGS THAT MATTER MOST

1. Swedenborg, *Heaven and Hell,* 278–83.

2. Perry, "'In the World,'" 13.

3. Ring, *Heading toward Omega,* 96.

4. Unnamed author, quoted in Flynn, *After the Beyond,* 88.

5. Unnamed author, quoted in Rogo, *Return from Silence,* 195–96; emphasis added.

6. Unnamed author, quoted in Grey, *Return from Death,* 53.

7. Unnamed author, quoted in Ring, *Heading toward Omega,* 55.

8. Ritchie, *My Life after Dying,* 29.

9. Patrick, quoted in Ring, *Heading toward Omega,* 40.

10. Brigham Young, in *Journal of Discourses,* 14:221.

11. See Heber C. Kimball, in *Journal of Discourses,* 4:135–36.

12. Grey, *Return from Death,* 54.

13. In McDonagh, *Journal of Near-Death Studies,* Vol. 8, no. 1 (Fall 1989), 56.

14. See Orson Pratt, *The Seer* 1, no. 10 (October 1853): 156–57.

15. See ibid.

16. Ballard, *Melvin J. Ballard,* 66.

CHAPTER 8: LIVING TO DIE

1. *Teachings of Harold B. Lee,* 75; emphasis added.

2. Epictetus, *Golden Sayings,* 161.

3. Packer, *Mine Errand from the Lord,* 50.

4. *Teachings of Howard W. Hunter,* 15–16.

5. Shakespeare, *Measure for Measure,* 3.1.5–6. References are to act, scene, and lines.

6. *Teachings of Gordon B. Hinckley,* 622–23.

7. Ibid., 624; emphasis added.

8. Spencer W. Kimball, *Miracle of Forgiveness,* 100.

9. *Teachings of Spencer W. Kimball,* 173.

10. Spencer W. Kimball, quoted in Gardner, "Finding Joy in the Savior's Plan," 73.

11. Orson Pratt, in *Journal of Discourses,* 3:105.

12. Bryant, *Thanatopsis and Other Poems,* 14.

13. Hinckley, "The Empty Tomb Bore Testimony," 66.

WORKS CITED

Atwater, P. M. H. *Coming Back to Life*. New York: Dodd, Mead & Co., 1988.

Ballard, Melvin J. *Melvin J. Ballard—Crusader for Righteousness*. Salt Lake City: Bookcraft, 1966.

Benson, Ezra Taft. *The Teachings of Ezra Taft Benson*. Salt Lake City: Bookcraft, 1988.

Bryant, William Cullen. *Thanatopsis and Other Poems*. New York: Effingham Maynard & Co., 1884.

Cannon, George Q. *Gospel Truth: Discourses and Writings of George Q. Cannon*. 2 vols. in 1. Edited by Jerreld L. Newquist. Salt Lake City: Deseret Book, 1987.

Crowther, Duane S. *Life Everlasting*. Salt Lake City: Bookcraft, 1967.

Emerson, Ralph Waldo. *Representative Men: Seven Lectures*. London: George Routledge & Co., 1850.

Epictetus. *The Golden Sayings of Epictetus*. Vol. 2, pt. 2. Translated by Hastings Crossley. The Harvard Classics. New York: P.F. Collier & Son, 1909–14; Bartleby.com, 2001. Available at www.bartleby.com/2/2/; accessed 15 February 2012.

Faust, James E. "Dear Are the Sheep That Have Wandered." *Ensign,* May 2003, 61–68.

First Presidency [Joseph F. Smith, John R. Winder, and Anthon H. Lund]. "The Origin of Man." *Improvement Era,* November 1909, 75–81; reprinted in *Ensign,* February 2002, 26–30.

Flynn, Charles P. *After the Beyond.* Englewood Cliffs, NJ: Prentice-Hall, 1986.

Gardner, Wilma. "Finding Joy in the Savior's Plan." *Ensign,* March 1988, 73.

Grey, Margot. *Return from Death.* London: Arkana, 1987.

Hale, Heber Q. "Everyone Had Something to Do." Quoted in Lee Nelson, *Beyond the Veil,* 2 vols. Springville, UT: CFI, 2011, 1:47–58.

Harris, Barbara, and Lionel C. Bascom. *Full Circle: The Near-Death Experience and Beyond.* New York: Pocket Books, 1990.

Hinckley, Gordon B. "The Empty Tomb Bore Testimony." *Ensign,* May 1988, 65–68; used by permission.

———. *The Teachings of Gordon B. Hinckley.* Salt Lake City: Deseret Book, 1997.

Hunter, Howard W. *The Teachings of Howard W. Hunter.* Edited by Clyde J. Williams. Salt Lake City: Bookcraft, 1997.

———. "The Gospel—A Global Faith." *Ensign,* November 1991, 18–19.

International Association of Near-Death Studies Conference, Georgetown University, Washington, DC, 15 August 1990, Experiencers Panel Discussion (transcript by author), 6–7.

Journal of Discourses. 26 vols. London: Latter-day Saints' Book Depot, 1854–86.

Kimball, Spencer W. *The Miracle of Forgiveness.* Salt Lake City: Bookcraft, 1971.

———. *The Teachings of Spencer W. Kimball.* Edited by Edward L. Kimball. Salt Lake City: Bookcraft, 1982.

Larson, A. Karl, and Katherine Larson, eds. *Diary of Charles Lowell Walker.* Logan, UT: Utah State University Press, 1980.

Lee, Harold B. *The Teachings of Harold B. Lee.* Edited by Clyde J. Williams. Salt Lake City: Bookcraft, 1996.

Maxwell, Neal A. *Notwithstanding My Weakness.* Salt Lake City: Deseret Book, 1981.

———. "Patience." *1979 Devotional Speeches of the Year: BYU Devotional and Fireside Addresses.* Provo, UT: Brigham Young University Press, 1979.

McDonagh, John M. "Book Review: *After the Beyond: Human Transformation and the Near-Death Experience,* by Charles P. Flynn." In *Journal of Near-Death Studies,* Vol. 8, no. 1 (Fall 1989), 55–57.

Millet, Robert L. *When a Child Wanders.* Salt Lake City: Deseret Book, 1996.

Millet, Robert L., and Joseph Fielding McConkie. *The Life Beyond.* Salt Lake City: Bookcraft, 1986.

Moody, Raymond A., Jr. *Life after Life: The Investigation of a Phenomenon—Survival of Bodily Death.* Toronto: Bantam Books, 1975.

———. *Reflections on Life after Life.* New York: Bantam Books, 1977.

———. *The Light Beyond.* New York: Bantam Books, 1989.

Morse, Melvin, with Paul Perry. *Transformed by the Light: The Powerful Effect of Near-Death Experiences on People's Lives.* New York: Villard Books, 1992.

Packer, Boyd K. *Mine Errand from the Lord: Selections from the Sermons and Writings of Boyd K. Packer.* Salt Lake City: Deseret Book, 2008.

———. *Teach Ye Diligently.* Salt Lake City: Deseret Book, 1975.

Palmer, Spencer J. *The Expanding Church.* Salt Lake City: Deseret Book, 1978.

Peale, Norman Vincent. "There Is No Death." *Plus: The Magazine of Positive Thinking.* March 1991, 7–9.

Perry, L. Tom. "'In the World.'" *Ensign,* May 1988, 13–15.

Pratt, Orson. *The Seer.* 2 vols. Washington, DC: Franklin D. Richards, October 1854.

Pratt, Parley P. *Key to the Science of Theology: A Voice of Warning.* Salt Lake City: Deseret Book, 1965.

Rawlings, Maurice. *Beyond Death's Door.* New York: Bantam Books, 1978.

Ring, Kenneth. *Heading toward Omega: In Search of the Meaning of the Near-Death Experience.* New York: William Morrow and Company, 1985.

———. "Amazing Grace: The Near-Death Experience as a Compensatory Gift." *Journal of Near-Death Studies* 10, no. 1 (Fall 1991): 11–40.

Ring, Kenneth and Sharon Cooper. *Mindsight: Near-death and Out-of-body Experiences in the Blind.* Palo Alto, CA: William James Center for Consciousness Studies, 1999.

Ritchie, George G., Jr., M.D. *My Life after Dying: Becoming Alive to Universal Love.* Norfolk, VA: Hampton Roads Publishing, 1991.

Ritchie, George G., Jr., with Elizabeth Sherrill. *Return from Tomorrow.* Waco, TX: Chosen Books, 1978.

Rogo, D. Scott. *The Return from Silence: A Study of Near-Death Experiences.* Wellingborough, Northhamptonshire, England: Aquarian Press, 1989.

Sabom, Michael B. *Recollections of Death: A Medical Investigation.* New York: Harper & Row, 1982.

Shakespeare, William. *Measure for Measure.* In *William Shakespeare: The Complete Works, Second Edition,* ed. Stanley Wells and Gary Taylor. Oxford: Clarendon Press, 2005.

Smith, Joseph. *History of The Church of Jesus Christ of Latter-day Saints.* Edited by B. H. Roberts. 7 vols., 2d ed. rev. Salt Lake City: The Church of Jesus Christ of Latter-day Saints, 1932–51.

————. *Joseph Smith* [manual]. In Teachings of the Presidents of the Church series. Salt Lake City: The Church of Jesus Christ of Latter-day Saints, 2007.

————. *Teachings of the Prophet Joseph Smith*. Selected by Joseph Fielding Smith. Salt Lake City: Deseret Book, 1976.

Smith, Joseph F. *Gospel Doctrine*. Salt Lake City: Deseret Book, 1986.

————. In Conference Report, April 1916, 1–8.

Snow, Lorenzo. "Discourse by President Lorenzo Snow." *Millennial Star* 56, no. 4 (1894): 49–53. Quoted in Dale C. Mouritsen, "The Spirit World, Our Next Home." *Ensign*, January 1977, 46–50.

Swedenborg, Emanuel. *Heaven and Hell*. Translated by George F. Dole. New York: Swedenborg Foundation, 1990.

Woodruff, Wilford. *Discourses of Wilford Woodruff*. Selected by G. Homer Durham. Salt Lake City: Bookcraft, 1946.

Young, Brigham. *Discourses of Brigham Young*. Compiled by John A. Widtsoe. Salt Lake City: Deseret Book, 1966.

————. Brigham Young Collection. Available at www.josephsmith .net >Resource Center >Documents >Other >Brigham Young Collection, February 17, 1847; accessed on 10 February 2012.

Zaleski, Carol. *Otherworld Journeys: Accounts of Near-Death Experience in Medieval and Modern Times*. Oxford: Oxford University Press, 1987.

INDEX